You Can Minister in the Spiritual Gifts

By Fran Lance
with JoAnne Sekowsky

Free Lance Ministries
PO Box 7169
Seattle, WA 98133

You Can Minister in the Spiritual Gifts

Tongues

Interpretation

Prophecy

The Word of Knowledge

The Work of Wisdom

Discerning of Spirits

Faith

Healing

Miracles

ISBN 0-9623908-1-X

Dedication

To the Rev. Canon Dennis Bennett and his wife, Rita, who
have been faithful to teach and minister in the spiritual gifts.

Contents

Foreword

I'll never forget the day Fran Lance first appeared on my doorstep. It was 1971. I had just been newly baptized in the Holy Spirit at St. Luke's Episcopal Church in Ballard where Fr. Dennis Bennett was the rector.

Those were exciting days. The Holy Spirit was moving in ways I had never witnessed, even though I was raised in a pastor's home. Everything was new to the many of us from mainline denominational churches, who were experiencing Pentecost for the first time. We were all so hungry for more of God and eager to learn.

A group of about 80 women met in my home on a weekly basis. Shade O'Driscoll, the co-rector's wife from St. Luke's, had graciously agreed to teach us for a season. I opened my door to greet her the first day of our meeting, and there stood Fran, a friend I hadn't seen since college days. With open hearts we began the meeting with Fran and Shade sharing with us what the Lord had given them. It was there I first heard about the gifts of the Spirit and that they were for today! Fran's teaching on the gifts was excellent, so balanced, so attainable. It wasn't something for just a select few. Jesus wanted to be able to speak, bless, encourage, and edify. And He wanted to do it through His Body, His people.

Through the years, Fran's prophetic gifting and ability to move in the Spirit has blessed and encouraged untold thousands. I know you, too, will be inspired as you read this book.

Jane Hansen
President of Women's Aglow, International

Introduction

"Time to eat," I called out. Our five little children ran from various corners of the house to be seated at the kitchen table. I asked the usual question, "Did you wash your hands?" The kitchen was suddenly quiet as the guilty ones tried to brush off the dirt. I knew this was a perfect opportunity to teach.

I asked a second question, "Why should you wash your hands before you eat?" The kitchen was even more quiet as the children thought about this question. Finally our four-year-old Chad smiled a big smile and blurted out his answer, "So we don't get our forks dirty."

It was hard not to laugh, but I knew Chad wasn't trying to be funny. He had never really thought about my question before so when I asked him for an answer, he just said whatever came to mind. In one way, his answer wasn't wrong, but it wasn't close to what I was hoping one of the children would give. He lacked knowledge and it was my responsibility to give him that knowledge.

The Bible says, "My people perish for lack of knowledge."

As a missionary in my twenties, I lacked knowledge, too. I thought I was well-trained—I had my bachelor's degree from a Christian college, a teaching certificate, and some seminary classes—but I knew nothing about the gifts of the Holy Spirit.

One time one of my students asked me what had happened in the Book of Acts. What about speaking in tongues and healing? What about miracles? Could we expect those things to happen now? I gave an answer that today sounds like Chad's answer: "So we don't get our forks dirty." My answer wasn't totally wrong but it was far from right. I said that God could repeat the book of Acts today, but we don't really see it happening. My intention was to make sure she didn't get her hopes up and be disappointed. However, for years my answer haunted me. I knew it wasn't right, but I didn't know the correct answer.

I'm sure Chad, who is now 26 years old, knows why he needs to wash his hands before he eats. Life teaches us if we want to learn. I've learned during those years, too—I've learned that God is the same today as He was in the book of Acts. He is a miracle-working God. He still heals physically, emotionally and spiritually.

Knowledge of the gifts of the Holy Spirit in 1 Corinthians, chapters 12, 13, and 14 opened my eyes to truth I had never known before. I see in God's Word that from the beginning God chose to let us work along side Him or co-labor with Him as the Scriptures say. He allowed Adam, the first man, to co-labor with Him by giving names to the animals. God created the animals and Adam named them. Notice that God did the hard part and Adam did the easy part. It is still the same today. God does the supernatural part and we do the natural part. We pray or lay hands on the sick and God heals. We cannot do God's part but very often He requires us to do something—pray, believe, anoint with oil, forgive—before He does His part.

The gifts of the Holy Spirit are our tools to use as we co-labor with Him! As I've traveled in the United States, Canada and Europe I've been struck time and time again how many Christians—leaders and laymen alike—don't know how to minister in the gifts of the Spirit. Oh, they could probably recite the list of gifts if asked, but when it comes to using them in their ministry, to be channels of God's grace, blessing, and His healing—they strike out. They just don't know what to do.

It is my desire to teach others how to be co-laborers with God. If you aren't certain how to do this, then I pray that this book will be used to teach you. God bless you as you learn.

Fran Lance
Summer, 1994

Chapter One

My Introduction to the Gifts of the Holy Spirit

The words the white haired woman spoke came with such power and love that I found myself trembling. Was this the gift of prophecy I had heard about? Did this woman actually hear from God? Could she deliver a prophetic message to me the way she had to several of my friends?

Those thoughts were quickly replaced by another kind. Did I really want her to speak to me? What would God have to say? Would the message embarrass me? Would God scold me in front of the other women? Would He reveal all the sins I had committed in my 33 years? Or would He tell me to go to the jungles of Africa to serve Him? What would I do if He did?

Curiosity and spiritual hunger had drawn me to this home

meeting near my house. Although I had been baptized in the Holy Spirit for several months, I knew little about the spiritual gifts except through my reading. My Baptist background made me cautious. I didn't want to get mixed up in anything "strange" unless I was sure it came from the Lord. Still, I could no longer fight my spiritual hunger for more of God and His power. I wanted to serve the Lord and see the results that the early Christians experienced.

So here I sat at this home meeting, cautious and ready to run at the first appearance of anything strange.

Sister Woodward might go unnoticed at the supermarket, but as I listened to her preach and prophesy that morning, I really sat up and took notice. There was something about this 65-year old woman in her white dress, with a flower pinned on her left lapel, her white hair tied in a bun. Of course, she carried a huge black King James Bible. Her face was a little stern, but when she smiled, her gentle spirit showed through. She glowed with the presence of Jesus.

I looked around the room at the women sitting there, some of whom I knew. My but they were quiet!

As Sister Woodward preached, the tension that filled the room faded. Everyone there knew we were in the presence of Jesus.

After awhile she began to prophesy over several of the women. I was captivated by the love of God that came from her lips. "Hold fast to My hand and rest in My love," she told one woman. "I have you in My intensive care. My concern for you is deeper now than when things are normal. Draw upon the resources of My grace."

She prophesied to another woman: "Have I not told you to

feed upon My Word so that you may be strengthened by My strength? I will give you wisdom as you depend on Me and not on your own intellect."

Some women smiled happily as they heard their "word" from the Lord; others burst into tears, but I could tell that each woman was deeply moved by what Sister Woodward said to her.

Although Sister Woodward didn't prophesy to me that day, I felt blessed just watching and listening to her minister God's grace and love.

A word of prophecy to me

I attended other meetings and one day Sister Woodward prophesied over me: "Fran, I see you with a suitcase and you're traveling all over the world. You're dressed in a tweed suit and you're taking giant steps like a woman who knows where she's going and is determined to get there. The day will come when you are out more than you are in (at home), preaching, teaching and ministering God's power."

When she spoke, I knew her words were from God. What I didn't know was that it would be 18 years before these words came true—after my five children were grown—after I had learned to move in power in the spiritual gifts at home.

My background

I first become aware of the lack of power in my life when my husband Russ and I taught at a mission school for two years in Alaska. The students, mostly Indians, Eskimo and Aleut came from all over Alaska to board at our school. My teaching fields were home economics and physical education, which gave me exceptional opportunity to get very close to my students. Although I was only in my twenties, some of them looked to me as "Mom."

How I desired to create a hunger in their hearts to know Jesus. However, no matter how hard I tried to do this, most of them had little interest in spiritual things.

Russ and I had gone to Alaska with such high hopes, but these two years working with young people turned out to be a discouraging time for us. Although a few did become Christians, we stood powerless as we watched them slip away.

"Russ, what are we doing wrong? Why aren't kids who become Christians living Christian lives?"

"I wish I knew," he replied.

Although my husband and I had many similar conversations, this was as far as it ever went. We blamed ourselves, trying to find a reason for the things that were going wrong in our lives.

Often at night I cried out to God for some answers.

Our new baby—God help!

Disillusioned and disappointed, Russ and I returned to Seattle. Three years before, a series of tests followed by a medical consultation had told us there was only the slimmest possible chance of my getting pregnant. That slim chance had kept me going but now I knew there wasn't going to be a baby, no matter how badly I wanted one. In Seattle we adopted our first child, Dirk.

The awesome responsibility of a baby of my own to train

and nurture in the things of God created in my heart a longing for a deeper relationship with the Lord. But I didn't know how to obtain that relationship. I was obedient to all I knew. Russ and I were active members of a Baptist church and Russ taught and coached at Kings Christian School in Seattle. I had a weekly prayer meeting for other mothers in our home. We were also temporary parents to five high school students from out of state who attended Kings. Since we lived on campus I was very active as a volunteer counselor. The kids seemed to just "drop in" and want to talk. I wished I had "more" to give them but I didn't know what that "more" would be.

The baptism in the Holy Spirit

I shared my longing with a new friend, Pat. She just smiled. "Fran," she said, "I know what you're looking for—the baptism in the Holy Spirit.

The baptism in the Holy Spirit? What was that? And why hadn't I heard about it at my church if it was the solution to all my problems?

Pat shared her own personal testimony and told how this experience opened a new love relationship with the Lord.

Even after hearing her testimony, I felt slightly offended to think she felt I needed more than I already had. After all, I'd gone to a Christian college and been a missionary. But I swallowed my pride and listened to her.

She also told me about an Episcopal priest in the Seattle area, Fr. Dennis Bennett, who taught on the baptism in the Holy Spirit and even prayed for people to receive it.

The minute she said St. Luke's Episcopal Church, my defenses went up. I realized I had heard about this church before and about the Holy Spirit movement that was going on there. As a good Baptist, I wasn't sure I should even visit that church. Still, as I thought it over, the baptism in the Holy Spirit sounded so much like what I was looking for that I went to see for myself.

My first experience at St. Luke's was another disappointment. I went to the altar to be prayed for, but I didn't experience the joy that people said I would have. Yes, I did say a few words I didn't understand and the people praying for me said I was praying in tongues, but I didn't believe them. The whole experience left me with an uncomfortable, almost angry, feeling towards St. Luke's.

A friend, Joyce, took me to another meeting to hear Rita Bennett, Dennis Bennett's wife, teach on this subject. I was impressed with her knowledge of Scripture and when I got home I checked out everything she had said in my own Bible.

That night I knelt by my bed and asked the Holy Spirit to give me a new language and after awhile I made a few sounds. Was I really speaking in tongues? I wasn't sure. I got up and wrote down the sounds I was making. At the baby's three o'clock feeding, I tried again. This time I got another word. I wrote it down.

The next morning I went to see still another friend, Connie. Before I could say anything, she said, "The Lord has revealed to me that you are baptized in the Holy Spirit and speak in tongues."

By this time I was beginning to believe that perhaps I really had been baptized in the Holy Spirit, but these few sounds I made certainly didn't sound like the fluent language that flowed out of the mouths of my friends.

At a prayer meeting one morning, Joyce said, "Let's pray for a release of Fran's prayer language. She would like to speak more fully in tongues."

I wanted to drop through the floor in my embarrassment, but as the women prayed, I felt a release in my spirit and my embarrassment was gone. Words, new beautiful words, began to flow out of me. I felt a newness, a cleanness I had never felt before. I felt joy.

Missing equipment

As I thought about this new experience in the days that followed, I realized that my missionary time had been a disappointment because I hadn't been fully equipped to do the job. I had needed the power of the Holy Spirit to do the work of a missionary. I had needed the release of the Holy Spirit to have a closer relationship with the Lord.

Reading my Bible, I began to see that the gifts of the Holy Spirit in 1 Corinthians 12 are the tools God gives us to do His work. In my college and seminary experience, I hadn't been taught about these beautiful gifts God wants all Christian to have.

I knew there was much more for me to learn, and I was so eager to learn it. I asked God to teach me. His answer to my prayers came that significant day when a friend invited me to her home meeting to hear Sister Woodward preach and prophesy.

Other teachers

During this time, God raised up many teachers in the Body of Christ. God was satisfying not only my own but the hunger of thousands of people who were not being taught about the Holy Spirit in their own churches. Cassette tape recorders appeared on the market, and I listened to hundreds of Bible teaching tapes, taking careful notes so I would learn all I could.

I learned much. Most of all, I learned that God wanted to equip and use all of us in ministry. My prayer became, "Equip me, Lord."

Chapter Two

Salvation and the Baptism in the Holy Spirit

Our Christian experience begins with salvation. Ministering in the gifts begins with the baptism in the Holy Spirit.

I realize that most people reading this book are already saved and baptized in the Holy Spirit. However, I'm going to present the material in this chapter just the way I do at my seminars. When you minister in the gifts, it is essential that you make sure the people you pray for either have or are ready to receive salvation and the baptism in the Holy Spirit. You can use this material as you lead them into these two wonderful experiences.

Salvation

Sometimes we like to make salvation complicated, but

Scripture gives only four requirements:

1. Repentance
   "Repent and be baptized every one of you, in the name of Jesus Christ for the forgiveness of your sins," (Acts 2: 38).

2. Belief in Christ
   "Believe in the Lord Jesus , and you will be saved" (Acts 16:31).

3. Confession
   "If you confess with your mouth, 'Jesus is Lord,' and believe in your heart that God raised him from the dead, you will be saved," (Rom. 10: 9).

4. Baptism
   "Whoever believes and is baptized will be saved" (Mark 16:16)[1].

Acts 2:21 tells us, *"Everyone who calls on the name of the Lord will be saved."* Often the first step in becoming a Christian is simply to cry out for help.

Many wonderful things happen to us when we become Christians.

1. We are spiritually reborn. (John 3:3).

2. God comes to live in our spirits so we are never alone again (1 Cor. 6: 17).

3. We are turned from darkness to light, from the power of Satan to God (Acts 26:18).

4. We have been rescued from the dominion of darkness and transferred into the kingdom of light (Col. 1:13).

5. Our sins are forgiven (Acts 3:19) and God no longer remembers them (Ps. 103: 12).

Receiving God's salvation and forgiveness

If you are not yet a Christian, these are the steps to take to receive God's salvation and forgiveness.

1. Admit that you have been going in the wrong direction and are now willing to go God's way.

2. Pray and ask Jesus to come into your life to be your personal Savior and Lord.

3. Believe He has come into your life and thank Him for taking away your sin and guilt.

The following prayer is one I use in leading people to the Lord:

Dear Father,

I know I am a sinner, but I believe that Jesus Your Son died on the cross to clean away my sin and guilt. I believe that He physically rose from the dead to give me salvation. Lord Jesus, I put my trust in You. Come into my life. I receive You as my Savior and Lord, and I ask You to wash away my sins. Thank you, Jesus. I know You are living in me now. Amen.

Receiving the baptism in the Holy Spirit

John the Baptist said, *"The man on whom you see the Spirit come down and remain is he who will baptize with the Holy Spirit"* (John 1:33). We know that the person described here is Jesus. Jesus is the one who baptizes us with the Holy Spirit.

When we receive salvation, the Holy Spirit comes into our spirit (1 Cor. 6:17). In salvation, we "get" the Holy Spirit, but in the baptism in the Holy Spirit, He "gets" us! He is no longer confined to our spirit but is released to all of us even our tongues, which James describes as "restless evil, full of poison" (Jas. 3:8). The power of the Holy Spirit enables us to speak in a language we have not learned.

Renouncing the occult

There are two spirit worlds—one, evil; one, holy. Before you pray for the baptism in the Holy Spirit it is necessary to renounce any involvement in the evil spirit world.

Scripture warns us to stay away from that world. In Deuteronomy 18: 10-13, the Lord, through Moses says,

Let no one be found among you who sacrifices his son or daughter in the fire, who practices divination or sorcery, interprets omens, engages in witchcraft, or casts spells, or who is a medium or spiritist or who consults the dead. Anyone who does these things is detestable to the Lord, and because of these detestable practices the Lord your God will drive out those nations before you. You must be blameless before the Lord your God.

Here is a sample list of some ways doors are opened into the evil spirit world.

1. Cults—a religious group that teaches some other way to God than through Jesus Christ and His shed blood for forgiveness of sins

2. Mind-science groups

3. Reincarnation

4. Fortune-telling—crystal balls, palm reading, card reading, Ouija boards

5. Extrasensory perception—telepathy, clairvoyance, water witching or dowsing, pendulums

6. Astrology/horoscopes

7. Mind expansion drugs, hypnotism, transcendental meditation

8. Sorcery or witchcraft

9. Levitation, astral projection

10. Spiritism or spiritualism—trying to contact the dead.

If you are not cleansed from the evil spirit world, you may get into much confusion. You may hear a voice from that world and think it is God speaking. Some have said to me, "But Fran, I didn't really believe in it or it was just a game." Don't be deceived, get cleansed.

Ask the Lord to reveal to you any times you were involved in the evil spirit world. Then repent and ask Him to take away any effects this sin may have caused. Here is a sample prayer:

Dear Father,

Forgive me if I have been involved in anything contrary to Your Word. I renounce (name the cult or false teaching). In Jesus' name I put all these things under the blood of Jesus Christ and cast them into outer darkness, never to return again. Lord, fill those empty spaces with Your Spirit. In Jesus' name, Amen.

It is important to burn any books, games, statues, or other materials that were used in connection with this involvement.

I have prayed with many who had prayed for the baptism in the Holy Spirit but were unable to speak in tongues until they renounced their involvement in the evil spirit world.

Praying for the baptism in the Holy Spirit

Now you are ready to ask Jesus to baptize you in the Holy Spirit. This can be done anywhere, any time, when you are alone or with others. You may have others lay hands on you to receive, which is scriptural, but not necessary.

With the same childlike faith it took when you asked Jesus into your heart in salvation, ask Jesus now to baptize you in the Holy Spirit. A sample prayer would be:

Dear Lord,
I ask you to baptize me in your precious Holy Spirit
and give me a new language. Amen.

Ask, believe, and receive. Turn your whole heart to the Lord and begin to pray to Him, but not in English (or your native language) or in any language you already know. When the followers of Jesus received the Holy Spirit in Acts 2:4, there were three steps:

1. They were all filled with the Holy Spirit.

2. The Spirit enabled them so that

3. They began to speak in tongues.

All who were waiting and desiring the baptism got it. You are part of that "all" if you are seeking the baptism in the Holy Spirit. The early followers had to begin to speak. God did not force them. He won't force you, but if by faith you offer your lips and vocal chords to Him and begin to make sounds, the

Holy Spirit will give you a language. At first you may think you are making up the words. The devil tells most of us that lie. A two-year old may sound to us like he is making up words, but he knows what he is saying. Be childlike and receive. No child immediately has a fluent language and you probably won't either. You may remember from the first chapter of this book the difficulties I had.

Do you have to speak in tongues?

No one *has to* speak in tongues, but you *get* to. Note what the Bible says about tongues and you'll no longer ask that question.

1. "*He who speaks in tongues edifies himself*" (1 Cor. 14:4).

2. *"For anyone who speaks in a tongue does not speak to men but to God. . . . He utters mysteries with his spirit"* (1 Cor. 14:2). Speaking in tongues is speaking mysteries to God with our spirit. Often we don't know how to pray. We don't know what's really going on deep inside us.

3. Jesus said, "*These signs will accompany those who believe: In my name they will . . . speak in new tongues" (Mark 16:17)*.

4. The Apostle Paul said, "*I would like everyone of you to speak in tongues*" (1 Cor. 14:5).

5. Paul also said, *"I thank God that I speak in tongues more than all of you,"* (1 Cor. 14:18).

6. Paul went on to say, *"For if I pray in a tongue my spirit prays, but my mind is unfruitful. So what shall I do? I will pray with my spirit,* (in tongues) *but I will also pray with my mind* (his own language); *I will sing with my spirit, but I will also sing with my mind,"* (1 Cor. 14:14-15).

7. When you pray in tongues, you may be giving thanks and praising God (1 Cor. 14:16-17).

8. *"Build yourselves up in your most holy faith and pray in the Holy Spirit,"* (Jude 20).

9. *"The Spirit intercedes for the saints in accordance with God's will,"* (Rom. 8:27). We know when we pray in tongues we are praying a perfect prayer—a prayer that is God's perfect will.

10. Speaking in tongues is a powerful weapon against the devil's schemes. *"And pray in the Spirit on all occasions,"* (Eph. 6:18).

Speaking in tongues edifies us and makes us strong in the Lord. We can't help others if we aren't strong ourselves.

Notes

Some argue that it is not necessary to be baptized in water to be saved. They use the case of the thief on the cross who, as he hung dying next to Jesus, believed, repented, and confessed Jesus as his Savior. Obviously he never had a chance to be baptized. Likewise today, people receive Jesus on their death beds, in prisons or in other situations where they are unable to be baptized. God is a God of grace. He is not going to keep someone out of heaven if he cannot be baptized in water on earth. But Scripture makes it clear that we should make every effort to obey God wholeheartedly. If you are a Christian who has never been baptized in water, ask the Lord what He wants you to do. If you are really hearing Him speak, I believe He will tell you to be baptized. Obeying God always brings special blessings, and who doesn't need to be blessed by God?

Chapter Three

What are the Spiritual Gifts?

We're ready now to take a look at the spiritual gifts. Let's see what Scripture has to say about them.

Bible authorities tell us there are three major groups of spiritual gifts:

The motivational gifts
The ministry gifts
The manifestation gifts

The motivation gifts, which are found in Romans 12:4-8, are prophecy, service, ministry, teaching, encouragement, contributing to others, leadership and showing mercy. They reveal offices or ministries of the church.

The ministry gifts (Eph. 4:11-12) are apostles, prophets, evangelists, pastors and teachers. They reveal the authority of Jesus and they "prepare God's people for works of service, so that the body of Christ may be built up."

The manifestation gifts, given in First Corinthians 12:7-11, are tongues, interpretation of tongues, prophecy, word of wisdom, word of knowledge, discerning of spirits, faith, healing, and miracles. They reveal the power of Jesus. The manifestation gifts in turn can be divided into three groups:

The vocal gifts, which are the power to speak

1. Tongues

2. Interpretation of tongues

3. Prophecy

Revelation gifts (the power to know)

1. Word of wisdom

2. Word of knowledge

3. Discerning of spirits

Power gifts (the power to do)

1. Faith
2. Healings
3. Miracles

In this book we will concentrate mainly on the manifestation gifts.

Every time I return to First Corinthians 12-14, I'm surprised about how much Scripture has to say about the spiritual gifts.

Since there is an abundance of material available, why has the church as a whole largely neglected these gifts?

The excuse usually given is that the spiritual gifts were given for a limited time to help the church get established. I believe this is a lie of the enemy. Since the gifts are given to equip believers to do the work of God, it's easy to understand why Satan doesn't want us to know about them.

First Corinthians 12, 13, 14

Much of what we know about spiritual gifts is found in First Corinthians 12, 13 and 14. These three chapters have a lot to tell us.

1. We should not be ignorant about spiritual gifts (1 Cor. 12:1).

2. We are to eagerly desire spiritual gifts, especially the gift of prophecy (14:1, 39).

3. Although there are different kinds of gifts, they come from the same Spirit (12:4).

4. The gifts are given for the common good (12:7).

5. The Holy Spirit determines the giving of the gifts (12:11).

6. We are to eagerly desire the greater gifts (whatever gifts are needed for a specific time) (12:31).

7. At public meetings, all should come prepared to contribute (14:26).

8. Tongues edifies the one speaking (14:4).

9. Tongues with interpretation is equal to prophecy (14:5).

10. Those who speak in tongues (publicly) should pray for the interpretation (14:13).

11. When we pray in tongues, our spirit prays (14:14).

12. We should pray and sing with both the spirit and with the mind (14:15).

13. Paul prays frequently in tongues but in public he would rather prophesy (14:18-19).

14. Tongues are a sign for unbelievers (14:22).

15. Speaking in tongues should not be forbidden (14:39).

16. Prophecy leads the unbeliever to Christ (14:24-25).

17. Prophecy strengthens, encourages, and comforts (14:3).

18. Prophecy is for the believer (14:22).

19. Prophecy edifies the church (14:4).

20. The spirits of the prophets are subject to the control of the prophets (14:32).

21. Everything should be done in a fitting and orderly way (14:40).

22. The gifts should be accompanied by love. (13).

All Christians can minister

Scripture makes it very plain that all born-again Christians can minister these gifts from God to other people. God used Kathryn Kuhlman to inspire such faith in her audiences that many were healed at her meetings. She also had the gift of the word of knowledge so that she knew who was being healed of what ailment at a specific time.

I have already told you about how my friend, Sister Woodward, was used in the gift of prophecy. First, she would bring an anointed teaching from the Word of God, then she would go around the room and God would give her a prophecy for many individual members of the group. At times she would pray for physical healings or for family relationships. I knew the women very well in one group where Sister Woodward ministered and I also knew that she didn't know anything about the women's personal lives. Yet God spoke truth to them and brought comfort in their hurting areas. One day Sister Woodward prophesied that I would write. At that time I didn't even like to write a letter and yet now, 25 years later, I find myself with a pen in my hand quite often, actually enjoying writing. Her prophecy still inspires me, giving me the faith to do what God is asking of me.

There is no question that God wants us as Christians to be used in the gifts of the Holy Spirit. The gifts should be part of our everyday lives. We can expect them to be in operation when we invite our friends in for coffee, when we come together for family prayers, as well as when we are in a public meeting. After all, the gifts are merely part of the life of Christ expressed through us.

Minister in love

Our chief desire should be to minister the gifts in love. The kind of love needed is described in First Corinthians 13:4-8. Without it, the spiritual gifts may be used harshly and may hurt instead of heal. Love must be the vehicle by which the gifts are ministered to others.

God also warns us to study about how the gifts operate. We are not allowed short cuts. In fact, Paul calls us ignorant. Those are strong words but were surely true in my life when I first came into the baptism in the Holy Spirit. I got over my ignorance by hours of study, prayer, and practice in being a channel of the gifts.

In the first 12 years of my Christian life, I was not aware there were such beautiful gifts or tools for us to use as God's channels to bless others. Now I realize God wants to use each Christian in the gifts of the Holy Spirit. I encourage you to study how you can enter into that usefulness. God will decide the degree of anointing He will place upon you. In His sovereign will He anoints some people mightily, but we also may lay hands on the sick and expect them to recover. Others may not seem to have as strong a prophetic anointing as my friend but we may all prophesy. Step out in faith and leave the degree of anointing to the Lord.

Chapter Four

The Vocal Gifts

The 30 or so women gathered in my neighbor's living room were there for prayer and Bible study. We all had our heads bowed and one person at a time prayed. I had been to many prayer meetings in the 12 years I had been a Christian, and I thought this was just another regular meeting. The woman across the room from me began to pray, but after she had spoken a few words, I realized that she was praying in a language I didn't recognize. I didn't give it a second thought. Maybe she was from another country and couldn't speak English. After a short prayer in this unfamiliar language she stopped. There was a pause, and then from the other side of the room, a soft-spoken young lady said some beautiful comforting words. Somehow her words consoled me and drew me close to God. I felt as if He were right there in that room. Later, my friend told me that the woman who'd spoken in the language I didn't recognize was speaking in "tongues" and the lady who had spoken immediately afterwards had given the "interpretation" of the tongue.

A demonstration of two gifts

At this one meeting I had witnessed a demonstration of two of the three vocal gifts of the Holy Spirit listed in 1 Corinthians 12:7-11, the gift of tongues, which is speaking supernaturally in an earthly or heavenly language the person has not learned and the gift of interpretation, which is bringing the meaning of what was spoken in tongues.

Tongues as a devotional language

There are actually two expressions of tongues. One comes at the time we are baptized in the Holy Spirit. The release of the Spirit into every part of us is confirmed by our speaking in tongues. Our spirit speaks to the Father through the Holy Spirit without our human understanding interfering. We often call this type of speech our "prayer language" or "praying in the Spirit" and usually we use it for private communication with God. We may pray in tongues at any time we wish. We have complete control to start and stop at will, to speak softly, loudly, slowly or quickly, or even under our breath. It is something we decide to do and do not have to wait for the Holy Spirit to inspire us. By using it, our spirit is edified and our relationship with the Lord is kept fresh and vital. This kind of speaking in tongues may also be done in a group during a time of praise and worship and may be either spoken or sung.

The private expression of tongues does not need to be

interpreted. It is to edify the one speaking and to pray to God at a deeper level of prayer. Scripture calls this *"speaking mysteries"* in the spirit (1 Cor. 14:2). It is mysterious because the speaker doesn't know what she is praying. One learns with experience, however, to know the general purpose of the specific prayer time. For instance, if you are praising and worshipping the Lord in tongues, you may be very joyous. If you are interceding on behalf of someone else, you may become more serious and sense a groaning or compassion within your own spirit.

Many parents have been awakened in the middle of the night to pray for a child in trouble. My friend, Patty, awoke one night with a sense of urgency to pray for her son who was touring Mexico. After a time of ardent prayer, she felt released to go back to sleep. It was several months before she could ask her son what happened that night. The story he told was incredible. Hiking through Mexico, he was attacked by a motorcycle gang. Somehow he managed to escape them and make his way amid gunfire through a woods, finally coming to a walled area. He scaled the wall and then lay still till morning when he knew for sure his attackers were gone. Patty was able to determine that she had been awakened to intercede for her son at the exact time of the attack.

At times God will call a person into prayer for warfare against evil forces around the world and the prayer may come forcefully with tears and sobbing. If this happens to us, rather than being frightened by the intensity of our prayer, we should recognize the honor God bestows upon us when we express the very emotions and intercessions of His heart. Usually the person will pray in this manner for a time, then the feeling of urgency will pass and she can go back to her regular routine.

The gift of tongues

The gift of tongues in a public assembly, such as a church or a prayer meeting, has at least four purposes.

1. **Praise.** As you listen to a group of people corporately praying or singing in the Spirit, it is easy to recognize when they are praising. Each one prays or sings in a different language but praises God with his heart and words. Often tears of joy or thankfulness are seen on faces.

2. **Intercession.** This may happen as the congregation prays in tongues for a specific request. Intercession in tongues sounds more serious than praise.

3. **Rebuke.** This is cooperate prayer against evil forces. It may sound angry, but it is the Holy Spirit expressing His anger.

4. **Exhortation.** Exhortation in tongues is God speaking to His people a message of encouragement, strengthening or comfort.

Tongues in a group-setting is incomplete without the interpretation. When the gift of tongues is interpreted, the Church is edified.

Through the gifts of tongues and interpretation, God may be speaking to believers or to unbelievers. *"With foreign lips and strange tongues God will speak to this people"* (Isa. 28:11). Occasionally, a message given through the gift of tongues may be in a language understood by someone present in the meeting. This is one way God can get a special message to one He wishes to. The impact of the message, accompanied by the interpretation, is so strong that often that person, if an unbeliever, will acknowledge that it must have been God who spoke.

In their popular and instructive book, *The Holy Spirit and You*, Dennis and Rita Bennett tell the story of a Japanese war bride who came to this country following World War II. The couple were happy but the young woman, a Buddhist, resisted her husband's Christian faith. However, she did attend services with him, where she would pray her Buddhist prayers. As the couple knelt at the altar one evening, a woman kneeling beside them began to pray aloud in tongues. Suddenly the Japanese bride seized her husband's arm.

"'Listen!' she whispered in excitement. 'This woman speak to me in Japanese! She say to me: "You have tried Buddha and he does you no good; why don't you try Jesus Christ?" She does not speak to me in ordinary Japanese, she speak temple Japanese and use my whole Japanese name which no one in this country knows!' It is not surprising that the young lady became a Christian!"[1]

Interpretation of tongues

"Anyone who speaks in a tongue should pray that he may interpret" (1 Cor. 14:13.) Interpretation of tongues may come directly into the person's mind or by inspired thoughts, symbols, pictures, or scriptures. It is not a word by word translation but gives the general idea of what was said. On rare occasions, I have heard a person pray in tongues in a congregation without an interpretation following. This may have been a prayer in tongues to release the flow of the prophetic word or some other prayer to God. Those in charge of the meeting should

explain, if possible, what is happening. Usually a message in tongues is interpreted immediately following the tongue.

Those newly baptized in the Spirit cannot always distinguish between their prayer language and the gift of tongues. In their enthusiasm, they will sometimes think they are giving a message in tongues, when they are actually praising God. In this case someone else will give the interpretation or simply explain what the message is.

The gift of prophecy

The third vocal gift of the Holy Spirit is the gift of prophecy, the speaking forth of a message from the heart of God in one's own native language through the inspiration of the Holy Spirit. Its purpose is to strengthen, encourage, and comfort (1 Cor. 14:3) or build up, lift up, and cheer up God's people.

Recognizing the counterfeit

The world is fascinated with the idea of prophecy today. Stores specializing in crystals, taro cards, astrology paraphernalia, palmistry, and books about guiding spirits and demons proliferate the market place. In my own neighborhood two new stores have opened this past year plus a third store which sells a mixture of Christian and New Age publications. Fortune tellers and New Age channelers openly advertise their "talents." Turn on your TV set and you won't have to wait long before a guest will "prophesy" about the future of the world and about your favorite celebrity. Unfortunately for those who spend their time and money in these pursuits, they are all counterfeits of the Holy Spirit's gifts. Let us remember that Satan wants to destroy the power of God so we shouldn't be shocked when a counterfeit shows up. After all, Satan has been in the counterfeiting business for a long time and should be pretty good at it by now. Bankers and government agents study real money to become so familiar with every aspect of it that when a counterfeit comes through their hands, they recognize it. Christians should be so familiar with the real gifts from God that the counterfeit will be obvious. Let us as Christians study the real gift of prophecy so we will recognize it when we hear it and allow the Lord to bless us and others as we let this gift function in our meetings.

The main difference between the Holy Spirit's gift of prophecy and the counterfeit is the power source behind the gift. The power behind the counterfeit, which functions through psychic readers, crystal balls and Ouiji boards, is Satan. The power source behind the true gift of prophecy is God, the Holy Spirit. The satanic source eventually tears one down, brings much fear, guilt and condemnation.

The Holy Spirit's prophecy builds one up, brings peace, comfort, and a drawing near to God.

How prophecy comes

Prophecy may come as

1. Inspired thoughts
2. Pictures
3. Symbols
4. Scriptures inspired by God.

Three anointings of prophecy

The Bible describes three anointings of prophecy.

1. *The spirit of prophecy.* When the spirit of prophecy is present on a group, it is easy for anyone to prophesy (1 Cor. 14:31). In Acts 2:17 the prophet Joel is quoted, *"I will pour out my Spirit on all people. Your sons and daughters will prophesy."* Paul says in 1 Corinthians 14:31, *"For you can all prophesy in turn so that everyone may be instructed and encouraged."* In Revelation 19:10 we read, *"For the testimony of Jesus is the spirit of prophecy."* The spirit of prophecy is the words Jesus would say or testify. For example, "I love you"; "I will never leave you nor forsake you"; "You are the apple of my eye." These are words one may be inspired by the Holy Spirit to speak out when the spirit of prophecy is released by the Holy Spirit. Prophecy frequently contains scripture.

2. *The gift of prophecy.* The gift of prophecy is a deeper anointing than the spirit of prophecy. Sometimes, God uses a particular person to consistently minister prophecy; in fact, that person becomes known by others primarily as one who ministers in such a way. Others may minister this gift occasionally.

3. *The ministry of a prophet.* The third prophetic ministry we see is the *office* or *ministry* of the prophet. *"And in the church God has appointed prophets"* (1 Cor. 12:28). Prophets are called by God, not appointed by man. The office of the prophet has been God's voice throughout the Church Age to bring repentance, reformation, and restoration.

Prophecy as foretelling

Prophecy can be either a forth telling or a foretelling. Much of the Old Testament prophecy is foretelling, having to do with future events. For example many prophets, such as Isaiah, told of a day when the long-awaited Messiah would come to free Israel. These beautiful prophesies still bless us today.

> *For to us a child is born, to us a son is given, and the government will be on his shoulders. And he will be called Wonderful Counselor, Mighty God, Everlasting Father, Prince of Peace. Of the increase of his government and peace there will be no end. He will reign on David's throne and over his kingdom, establishing and upholding it with justice and righteousness from that time on and forever. The zeal of the Lord Almighty will accomplish this"* (Isa. 9: 6-7).

Or who has not been blessed by the archangel Gabriel's announcement to Mary:

> *"Do not be afraid, Mary, you have found favor with God. You will be with child and give birth to a son, and you are to give him the name Jesus. He will be great and will be called the Son of the Most High. The Lord God will give him the throne of his father David, and he will reign over the house of Jacob forever; his kingdom will never end"* (Luke 1: 30-33).

Today, although some prophecy foretells the future, much of what we hear in our churches or in private meetings is forth telling, such as this simple prophecy that was given to a local church at a time when many were greatly discouraged.

Man looks at the outside, but I, the Lord, look at your hearts. I know what is in your hearts and I am pleased with you. Be encouraged. You are going through a difficult time, but I am walking through it with you. I want you to know My joy in your difficult times. Be encouraged now in faith. I love you.

Through the gift of prophecy today God encourages and comforts both individuals and His church.

Notes

[1]Dennis and Rita Bennett, *The Holy Spirit and You* (Plainfield: Logos International, 1971), p. 86.

Chapter Five

Personal Prophecy

Last week a lady called me from the Portland, Oregon, area. She said, "Fran, about a year ago you prophesied that I would be ministering on TV. At the time I had no contact with television but within a few weeks I was invited to be on a program as a guest. Then I was asked by the station manager if I wanted to do a weekly program – a talk show of testimonies of what God had done in people's lives." She went on to say that she is now doing a weekly program and just loves doing it. When the opportunity came, the prophecy gave her faith that God was opening the door for her to do this ministry.

Personal prophecy is prophecy directed specifically at an individual. Keep in mind that it is a "gift." When someone gives me a prophecy I expect it to be a blessing from God. Yes, greater than any birthday or Christmas gift because it is God speaking directly to me to build me up, cheer me up, and comfort me.

Another word

A word given to me years ago said, "Fran, I see you have a row of cotton to hoe. When you get to the end of the row, you think you're finished, but the farmer assigns you another row. The Lord says He has seen you faithfully hoeing row after row and He is well pleased with you." The prophecy went on to say that the Lord had many fields of cotton for me to hoe but that He would always be there with me, strengthening me. Many times when I was tired, discouraged, and felt like I couldn't go on I've thought of those words. The prophecy strengthened and comforted me so I could complete the work God called me to do.

Another word that has encouraged me through the years was about intimidation. "Do not let unnecessary fears mount in your heart. You can stand tall and firm in Me. Don't let anyone intimidate you, especially men. They shall see the authority in you and this shall put an end to their dispute. I am giving you a new boldness." This prophecy let me know that the ministry God gave me may come under attack but I am not to back down. Those who attack will see God's authority in me, which will cause them to back off. I've needed those words many times. When I first began to minister, I was easily intimidated but God has given me boldness and courage. He is faithful to supply everything we need to accomplish the work He sends us to do.

Words of encouragement

I have two spiral notebooks filled with prophecies given to me over the years. Occasionally I will read them over. What a record of God's faithfulness! These prophecies were truly "gifts" to me. God continues to fulfill His word spoken in the prophecies year after year.

In 1972 this word was given to me: "Because of the strength of the union, many will be won to the Lord." My greatest desire has been to bring people to Jesus and this short little prophecy reminds me how that will be accomplished. I am to make sure that my relationship with God is strong, as that is how souls are saved. The first time I gave an altar call in Russia 33 people responded. I was amazed. You see, when I first started speaking I thought people would respond to the gospel because of my knowledge of the Bible and skill in presenting that word. Because I knew my limitations, that thought was scary. I wasn't a Bible scholar or a great orator. What courage I gained from those words – that it was in the strength of the union – my relationship with God that many would be won to the Lord. What a gift this prophecy has been to me.

Prophecy that predicts the future

In November 1974 I was speaking at an Aglow conference when a woman prophesied to me, "You're going to have a ministry that is very far reaching." Several people gave me similar prophecies throughout the years, but when this prophecy was given, I had five children at home and I rarely ministered. But a few years later doors began to open for me to minister, at first in the United States and Canada and then Europe. God began to prepare me while my children were growing up so that when they were out of the home and on their own, I was ready to go. When the invitations came, I already knew in my heart that it was God saying, "Now, go."

Prediction is a genuine part of prophecy, but only a small part. I find that many Christians expect a prophetic word to tell them what is in their future. They seem disappointed if God doesn't tell them what's ahead. One woman said, "Can you ask God if I will ever be married? I don't care when or to whom but I just want to know 'if.'" I told her that God had many ways to speak to her and that she should ask Him herself or just wait and see. I didn't want that responsibility.

Prophecies that don't seem to come true

Years ago I wanted to give birth to a baby. My prayer group knew my desire and we prayed about it often. In fact, I received many prophetic words from my friends that I would get pregnant. Russ and I had already adopted two children when we started praying, and I kept trusting God that I would get pregnant. Soon we had adopted five children, three boys and two girls. But I continued to pray. It wasn't until our five were well into Junior High and High School that I finally withdrew my prayer request.

What went wrong? Were the prophecies false? Didn't I have enough faith to make the words come to pass? I may not have the complete answer until I get to heaven, but I have learned a few things through this experience that I will share.

1. Friends love us and want to encourage us. That love may get in the way of really hearing God's voice.

2. The prophecies may be wrongly interpreted. While I was still praying to have a baby, a friend prophesied that God was going to give me my heart's desire. We all

interpreted that to mean God was going to give me the baby I wanted. However, another friend knew I had another heart's desire — to write a book, and she rightly interpreted the prophecy to say that God was going to give me that desire. That prophecy came true with the publication of my first book, *Fran,* which has been retitled, *Tell Your Secret.*

3. In my earliest prayer group after the baptism in the Holy Spirit, we often thought that if we had enough faith God would bring the answer. We struggled with this a lot, always looking at "our faith," trying to muster up more, repenting for not having enough. Trying, trying, trying. Then we learned that it wasn't Our Great Faith but God's Great Faithfulness. We learned to quit trying to twist God's arm and relax and let Him bring His will to pass.

4. Our early prayer group also learned to stay away from dates. Someone prophesied that a wayward husband would return to his family by March 25. We waited, prayed, and believed God to fulfill this word. The date came and went and this man didn't come home. We were really disappointed but after we learned to stay away from dates, he eventually accepted the Lord. However, he never returned to his family.

Prophecies that predict future events or ministries can degenerate into fortune-telling. As we said earlier, our nation is preoccupied with astrology, fortune-telling, spiritualism, clairvoyance and personalities like Jean Dixon and Edgar Cayce. Why this preoccupation? To know the future. As Christians we need to be very careful we don't get caught up in the world's ways.

Spiritual Abuses

The Bible says, *"God does nothing without revealing his plans to his servants the prophets"* (Amos 3:7). There is a legitimate knowing of the future as God speaks to the prophets and the prophets speak to the Church. But prophecies must be judged.

The Pentecostal movement, which began around the turn of the century, had a strong emphasis on personal prophecy. However, many abuses and problems arose in this movement because people were not taught to correctly judge the prophetic word. They didn't know that a word from God coming through an impure vessel can pick up words and ideas that aren't from God. They treated the prophetic word as though it were Scripture. Many were controlled by prophetic words that were not from God. Some insecure leaders (even pastors) controlled their people by "Thus saith the Lord," when the Lord had no part in the prophecy. Abuse of personal prophecy at that early date did more to curtail the work of the Spirit than anything else. We must learn from past experience to teach people the proper function of personal prophecy. We must give them permission to judge any prophetic word that is given to them.

Abuses Today

We still see abuse in personal prophecy today. This word was given to me 11 years ago: "Lay down your ministry or I will take it away from you . . . thus saith the Lord." When the woman finished prophesying to me, I thanked her for her efforts but then I said, "I can't receive this word as a word from God." I told her I had received numerous prophecies that God was expanding my ministry, not shutting it down. He was opening doors for me that I never dreamed He would. How could this woman be wrong? She was a Christian, one who called herself an intercessor and spent much time praying. Later I remembered that she had been in a class I taught on the "Gifts of the Holy Spirit." Because her words to individuals in the class were often hard and judgmental, I had corrected her several times. She hadn't received my counsel then but had allowed resentment to come in. That resentment resulted in the word, "Lay down your ministry." This is an example of the consequences of unconfessed sin. A person who is unwilling to be corrected and will not humble himself before God is an easy channel for Satan to use.

Despite my rejection of the woman's words, they still occasionally bothered me. I found myself thinking that maybe God *was* telling me to quit ministering. I had a friend pray with me for release. Then I remembered that the word had also said, "Or else I will take it away from you." I breathed a sigh of relief – I didn't have to worry. If I wasn't supposed to minister, God would take it away. More than 20 years have passed since I received that word and instead of taking away my ministry God has expanded it. The prophecy wasn't a word from God but a trick of the enemy to get me to give up.

Rusty pipes

Paul says, *"We have this treasure in jars of clay"* (2 Cor. 4:7). Prophecy that comes from God can still be affected by the person through whom it comes. Water may be pure at its origin but if the pipes carrying the water are rusty, the water will be colored, even contaminated, by the rusty pipes. The rust is not from the water but from the pipe. We may look at the one prophesying as a pipeline from God delivering His living water. However, if the person has unconfessed sin or lacks love, the water will be contaminated. That person's view of God as a hard judgmental God ready to pounce on His people if they make a mistake will affect the word also.

God works through imperfect humans, but the good news is that He is committed to perfect us if we are willing.

God's way is loving

A prophetic word may contain statements of a corrective or chastening nature. But when God speaks this way He does it in love and brings hope. If someone prophesies doom and destruction and consistently instills fear and never encourages or comforts, then you can be sure his words are not from God. I would not allow such a person to prophesy over me.

God wants to walk and talk with us in an individual, personal, intimate relationship. He does this today as we read and meditate on the Bible and as we let the Holy Spirit teach us. God has our calling, our work, planned for us before we are born. He called Samuel from birth to be a prophet, but Samuel had to learn. He didn't recognize God's voice at first but had to ask Eli what was going on. Samuel had to learn to distinguish the voice of God from other voices and from his own thoughts.

Timothy was told to stir up the gift or fan into flame the gift of God that was in him. The Bible goes on to say that God did not give him a spirit of timidity (2 Tim. 1:6-7). Evidently, he was being timid and this timidity was holding him back. I was timid when I first started out but as others ministered to me, especially by prayer and personal prophecy, I gained boldness. Personal prophecy spoken over me has been one of the most powerful gifts God has given me through the Body. I have truly been strengthened, encouraged, and comforted.

Chapter Six

How to Respond to the Prophetic Word

Some people are afraid to receive prophecy, afraid it will give them a problem with pride or lead them into error. Others are gullible, ready to believe any words another speaks to them. How then are we to respond to the prophetic words we hear spoken at our churches and meetings or are given to us individually? What should our attitude be when someone has a prophetic word for us?

How to judge prophecy

"Beloved, believe not every spirit, but try the spirits whether they are of God, because many false prophets are

gone out into the world" (1 John 4:1). The Bible tells us to test the spirits, and that includes the spirit behind any word of prophecy. I don't believe there are hard and fast rules for judging prophecy, but Scripture and experience give us guidelines we would be wise to follow.

1. Prophecy must agree with Scripture. The Spirit and the Word always agree (2 Tim. 3:16). God's truth in the Scriptures comes first. *"Watch your life and doctrine closely. Persevere in them"* (1 Tim. 4:16). Personal prophecy will never take the place of doctrine. Our foundation is the Scriptures. Anytime we follow prophecy more than the written word of God we are headed for trouble. Balance is the key here.

2. Prophecy must glorify and exalt Jesus. The Holy Spirit came to testify of Jesus (John 15:26, 16:14).

3. *"But the Spirit gives life"* (2 Cor. 3:6). Prophecy should give life and not death if it truly is of the Spirit. If a prophecy comes that is in direct contradiction to the Word of God or brings a pall over a meeting, the leader of the group must, in love, correct the situation. I remember sitting in a meeting a long time ago when a young man began to prophecy every time there was a silence. Many of his words were harsh and critical. What had been a joyful, sweet meeting quickly turned somber. Finally one of the elders corrected the young man, indicating that many of the things he was saying were not scriptural. Instead of accepting the correction, the young man abruptly left the meeting. Even after he was gone, it was hard to restore the sweet spirit

that had characterized the meeting earlier.

4. Prophecy should edify, exhort, and comfort or build up—lift up and cheer up (1 Cor. 14:3). It should be non-condemning. *"There is therefore now no condemnation to them that are in Christ Jesus"* (Rom. 8:1). A prophecy that condemns is not from the Holy Spirit and should be rejected. Whenever the Spirit rebukes or exhorts, He does it with tenderness and hope, causing one to be easily drawn to repentance in love (John 3:17). At times, a prophetic utterance that sounds condemnatory is just not completed. Perhaps the one prophesying became self-conscious and did not finish with the words of restoration. If this happens at a meeting you are attending, ask the Lord for the rest of the message. For instance, the Lord may be talking through a prophetic utterance about our sin, but He doesn't leave us condemned. He is full of grace and mercy and will always tell us how to correct the situation. If the prophecy stops short of hope, wait for the rest of the word. The Holy Spirit may speak it through another person, but don't be afraid to wait. Silence is often necessary so one can receive the message from the Holy Spirit.

5. Prophecy should be confirmed and/or be a confirmation of what God has already spoken to you (2 Cor. 13:1, Acts 13:2). It must always be confirmed by an inner witness.

6. The prophecy should be judged, not the person the prophecy is coming through (1 Cor. 13:9-10, Thess. 5:20-21).

7. Not every prophecy is for everyone hearing the words. God may not be talking to you in a particular message. Let those God is talking to receive it.

8. Trust the Holy Spirit in you. He promises to lead us into all truth. Don't be afraid to receive prophecy (John 16:13). It is 100% safe if one learns how to correctly judge it. Encourage the gifts in your meetings, but also teach your people how to judge them.

9. Those who prophesy are the best judges of prophecy (1 Cor. 14:29).

10. Prophecy should be communicated in a graceful manner. It should not be arrogant or legalistic.

Scripture gives us additional instructions concerning our attitude toward prophecy.

Hold onto the word God gives you

"Do not put out the Spirit's fire. Do not treat prophecies with contempt. Test everything. Hold onto the good" (1 Thess. 5:19-21). What wonderful instructions Paul gives us in these few words. The Word of God to you will boost your faith. When you first get a word, you may have difficulty believing that it is really from God. The prophetic word may be God telling you that you are the apple of His eye. That would be easy for some to believe, but not everyone. If you have had a lot of rejection in your life resulting in self-hatred or low self-esteem, you may find that Word hard to believe. A friend, Joan, was berating herself on the way to church, reminding the Lord of what a poor Christian she was and ending with the idea that God

couldn't possible love such an imperfect person. That morning at church, she received these words: "Stop condemning yourself. I don't see you the way you think. I see you only through the blood of My Son." These words from the Lord were the beginning of a change in the way Joan saw herself.

Exercise faith

Don't miss your blessing. Exercise faith by believing the Lord's words. When you receive a word that especially blesses you, write it out and tape it to your mirror. Repeat it aloud every time you see it. The word of God is powerful and eventually you will believe it and be healed of low self-esteem. You will be set free from self-hatred and further rejection. Confidence will increase so you can become what God wants you to be.

"Forget not all his benefits" (Ps. 103:2). Don't let God's word go in one ear and out the other. Prophecy is a benefit from God. It will edify, exhort, and comfort. I have written out most of the prophetic words given me. I have two notebooks filled with them. Sometimes I forget what God has said so periodically I read over these words to refresh my heart. I marvel at how God has fulfilled them. Some words are yet to be fulfilled; the things described may not happen for years. Don't try to fulfill the word in the flesh, but wait on God. Prepare yourself. Even while mothering five children, I prepared myself for the day God would send me to the nations. *"Forget not all His benefits."*

See your potential

The Scriptures say we can do all things through Christ

(Phil. 4:13). Don't look at what you are doing now but believe that God can and will equip you to do what He has spoken to you through the prophetic word.

Recently I gave a word to a young man that God would use Him in a creative way to bless others spiritually. The word went on to say that God would bring the finances he desperately needed through this creativity. A few months later he showed me how God fulfilled that word. He was marketing "miracle cups." When hot liquid is poured into the cups, a picture of Jesus appears on the outside of the cup. Each cup also has a special message. So far he has designed five cups, but I believe this is just the beginning. God wanted him to discover his potential as he acted on the word. He had to act. It cost him time, money, prayer, talent and faith to start, but how happy he is to see God at work through him.

Don't neglect the gift

"Do not neglect your gift which was given you through a prophetic message when the body of elders laid their hands on you" (1 Tim. 4:15). In this scripture Paul tells Timothy not to neglect his gift that came by way of the prophetic message. Satan is a thief so make sure you don't let him steal your words. Neglecting, forgetting, unbelief are all ways Satan can steal. Be aware of the thief and hold onto your word.

Conditional prophecies

If someone prophesies God's plan for you and you run from it, even though you know it is the truth, it will not come to pass. The Bible says, *"If you are willing and obedient, you will eat the best from the land"* (Isa. 1:19). The conditions are willingness to act upon and obedience to the word He gives you before God will bring to pass what has been prophesied.

Seemingly inaccurate prophecies

When Lazarus' friends brought word to Jesus of Lazarus' illness, Jesus said, *"This sickness will not end in death."* But Lazarus died. What do you think Jesus' disciples thought when they arrived and learned that Lazarus was dead? Do you think they thought that Jesus had really blown it? But when Jesus called Lazarus to come out of the tomb, he came. Yes, he died, but that was not the end of the story. Jesus raised him up again. Time had to pass before Jesus' words were fulfilled.

Sometimes God "voids" prophecy. Remember when Jonah pronounced a divine judgment on the city of Nineveh at the Lord's instructions: *"In forty days Nineveh will be destroyed"?* Was Nineveh destroyed? No! Why not? Because the people repented and sought God for mercy, and God stayed the city's judgment. Jonah's reaction to God's mercy was very human. He worried about his reputation. Here, he'd prophesied doom and destruction because God had told him to. Now God had accepted the people's repentance. What's a poor prophet to do with a God who behaves like that?

We must always be careful how we judge a prophetic word. God is a merciful God who will still cancel a pronouncement when there is repentance.

Exercise your authority over the devil

Paul told Timothy, *"So that by following them* (prophecies

said about him) *you may fight the good fight."* (1 Tim. 1:18). Many prophecies do not come to pass without our active cooperation. We may have to wrestle in prayer before a word can come to pass. If God said prophetically that He was going to restore your family, you may have to battle in prayer. You may need to not only confess the prophetic word to yourself but out loud to the devil before he eventually looses his grip on your family.

Eat the meat and spit out the bones

We all make mistakes, even people who prophesy. Hearers of the erroneous prophecy should quickly forgive and pray for the one who delivered the prophecy.

When you know a prophetic word is not God speaking, let it go. This isn't always easy. You may need others to pray for you. A wrong concept of God in the one prophesying can result in harsh rebuking words that you know is not God's voice. Pray for that person.

Sources of prophecy

Prophecy can come from one of three sources: the Holy Spirit, our human spirit or soul, or a satanic spirit.

We will all make mistakes when we begin to prophesy. Even Peter responded to a wrong spirit when his love for Jesus prompted him to rebuke Jesus for saying He must die (Mark 8:32-33). But this is the same Peter who cried, *"You are the Christ, the Son of the living God"* (Matt. 16:16).

If we make a mistake, we can only ask the Lord's forgiveness, move closer to Him, and go on.

Chapter Seven

The Revelation
Gifts

Listed in the newspaper were hundreds of names of people who had not claimed money which belonged to them in inactive bank accounts, savings accounts, unclaimed safety deposit boxes with precious jewelry and other valuables in them. Perhaps many of these people had died and the inheritance would go unclaimed. I found myself glancing over the names and secretly hoping a rich relative had left me a fortune. I didn't find my name on that list but how I wanted the missing people to see their names and claim their inheritances. It made me happy just to think abut people receiving an unexpected inheritance. I could visualize women redecorating their houses or buying a new wardrobe for work; men replacing old cars with smooth-running, dependable, low-gas-mileage ones; children getting needed braces for their teeth; families getting out of debt; maybe even a dream-come-true ocean cruise for some.

The fact is, however, that much of the money represented on the list would never be claimed. It wasn't that the people didn't want their inheritance; it was just that they didn't know they had one coming.

Our legacy

Did you know that Christians are mentioned in a will? I had been a Christian for 12 years before I heard about that will. I learned about it because someone read 1 Corinthians 12 to me. Mentioned in the will were the nine gifts of the Holy Spirit which are to bless me when I'm in need, nine gifts to bless others through me when they're in need.

First Corinthians 12 begins, *"Now about spiritual gifts, brothers, I do not want you to be ignorant."* *Ignorant* means you don't know about something. The people listed in the newspaper were ignorant of their inheritance. Jesus poured out the Holy Spirit from heaven when he ascended and blessed His church with gifts from above. Let us claim our inheritance as the Body of Christ.

In a previous chapter, we looked at the vocal gifts of the Holy Spirit: tongues, interpretation of tongues and prophecy. In this chapter we'll cover the three revelation gifts: the word of wisdom, the word of knowledge and the discerning of spirits (1 Cor. 12:8,10).

The word of wisdom

The word of wisdom is not the natural wisdom of man. It cannot be obtained by learning and becoming wise through the process of education. Rather, it is wisdom given supernaturally by the Holy Spirit at a particular time for a particular purpose. Notice we do not get a gift of wisdom but a portion of it—a word of wisdom. If we received the *gift* of wisdom we would never need to rely on God's *word* of wisdom. We would be wise all the time. However, God chose for us to be dependent upon Him, so by receiving only a word of wisdom we live in an expectancy that when we need it, the Holy Spirit will give it to us.

God gave Noah a word of wisdom in Genesis 6:13-14 when He said, *"I am going to put an end to all people, for the earth is filled with violence because of them. I am surely going to destroy both them and the earth. So make yourself an ark."* Noah obeyed and he and his family escaped the fate of the Earth. Noah received a directive from God and when he obeyed he was saved. God desires to continually give a word of wisdom to His people.

The word of wisdom often works very simply. My friend, Bonnie, had a very rebellious adult daughter, Carolyn. The young woman was so unpleasant much of the time that it was difficult to have a normal conversation with her, without a lot of harsh words being spoken. One day the Lord dropped a word of wisdom into Bonnie's heart. It was a very short message, only three words long: "Just love her."

Bonnie decided to act on the word the Lord gave her. The next time Carolyn dropped by, Bonnie told her how glad she was to see her and how nice she looked. The self-conscious little smile on Carolyn's face showed that the young woman was drinking in the loving words. For the next several months Bonnie saturated their relationship with all the loving words she could imagine the Lord saying to Bonnie. If Carolyn were unpleasant, instead of responding in kind, Bonnie replied in a loving way. And guess what? Within a short time the relationship between mother and daughter noticeably changed — all because Bonnie acted on the word of wisdom the Lord gave her.

The word of knowledge

The word of knowledge is not natural knowledge, but supernatural knowledge. It is not something of the intellect but a manifestation of the Holy Spirit. One does not increase in the word of knowledge through experience or intellectual pursuits. One receives it from the Spirit of God. He just drops the word into our spirit, and when He does this we know something He knows and wants us to know.

Jesus used the word of knowledge when He spoke to the Samaritan woman at the well, telling her about her life (John 4: 17), and Peter was acting on a word of knowledge when he confronted Ananias and Sapphira about their lying (Acts 5:3-4). Perhaps you have prayed and asked God to help you find a lost article and suddenly you knew where to look for it. The word of knowledge can come through a vision, an impression in the spirit, through a word God speaks to our spirit or through a dream.

The word of knowledge and the word of wisdom work hand in hand. The word of knowledge can be a fact that is supernaturally given by the Holy Spirit and then the word of wisdom may be given to direct one as to how to use that fact.

When I was a young mother I relied on the Lord to give me a word of knowledge and wisdom as I raised my children. I didn't want to be one of those snoopy suspicious mothers but I did want to know what was going on in my children's lives. The Lord was faithful through these two gifts not only to let me know when there was a problem but how to handle it correctly.

For example, one year I noticed that one of my sons, Chad, seemed unusually sad over a long period of time. His grades dropped and he seemed irritable and hard to get along with. As I prayed, the Lord seemed to say to me that Chad had a broken spirit. I wasn't even sure what a broken spirit was but at church the next Sunday one of the scriptures read defined a broken spirit as an abundance of sorrow.

I couldn't imagine any great sorrow Chad was going through but the Lord reminded me that we had just moved into a new home. This had been pure joy for me, but I began to see that for my 13-year-old it had been a real adjustment. Also, my boy had started a new school, and his life-long friends were no longer surrounding him. A boy who got great joy from people, he was having a particularly difficult time because he'd not had time to make new friends. For our other four children, the uprooting had gone smoothly, but for some reason this one boy was highly sensitive to change.

When God pointed out the problem, He showed me what I should do to help my son. I needed to give him extra grace, love, and patience. Within a few weeks he was his normal, happy self. Without the word of knowledge and the word of wisdom I could have handled the problem in a way that would have broken his spirit even more. Thank you, Lord, for the legacy you left me.

The discerning of spirits

The discerning of spirits is a supernatural revelation of the unseen spirit world. It gives one the ability to see or know the presence of a good spirit or the presence of an evil one. One may discern a spirit's presence or influence. The sense of the presence of the Holy Spirit brings joy, love, and peace. But discerning a wrong spirit brings heaviness and unrest. Paul discerned that the slave girl in Acts 16:17, even though she was saying true words, was speaking under the influence of the enemy. He commanded the spirit to leave and she was set free.

Discerning of spirits is not the same as natural discernment. Remember the gifts of the spirit are supernatural and cannot be learned. Natural discernment increases with maturity and knowledge. One may have great discernment but not be operating in the gift of discerning of spirits.

Early in my charismatic prayer meeting experiences I often heard people say, "Wasn't the presence of the Lord strong tonight?" I really didn't know what they were talking about. But not long after I was baptized in the Holy Spirit I, too, could sense the sweet presence of Jesus in a meeting.

For me, this was the beginning of discerning of spirits. Along with this experience I noticed that quite often when I was asked to counsel and pray with a person, the Holy Spirit would show me an evil spirit behind the person's problem. After the evil spirit was bound and cast out, the person was set free—delivered. During a deliverance prayer time, the gift of discerning of spirits is usually given to one or more persons involved in the prayer. We need God's knowledge when praying against evil powers.

Biblical examples

There are many examples of discerning of spirits in the Bible. Remember when Jesus told His disciples that He must die? What did Peter say? He said, "Never, Lord! . . . This shall never happen to you" (Matt. 16:22). Jesus discerned that Peter was speaking in a wrong spirit and pointedly told him so. Also, at the Last Supper, Jesus discerned that one of His chosen twelve had a wrong spirit and would betray him (John 13:21).

A friend, Doris, attended a prayer meeting which was co-led by two men, one of whom she knew. As soon as she entered the house, she began to feel uncomfortable, and the discomfort seemed to center around Dave, the leader she didn't know. Shortly into the meeting Dave walked over to her and said he had a word for her. Doris grew more uncomfortable. The "word" the man had for her was largely critical, as the man said the Lord found her to be a Christian lacking depth and she must change or suffer the consequences. The interesting thing was that the day before, Doris had been praying about that very thing and the Lord had assured her she was not a shallow Christian. Because of the word of knowledge the Lord had given her in advance and the discerning of a spirit not from Him, Doris was able to reject the prophesy. About a month later, she learned that the group had asked Dave to step down from leadership.

The gift of discerning of spirits is used to bring deliverance from evil spirits. It enables the ones praying to know if an evil spirit is present so they can cast it out and set the person free. This gift operates as a warning against false doctrine, false prophets, and false prophecies. You may have a check in your spirit. It's God's alarm system warning you to take action.

Judging the gifts

As you can see, any of these three gifts can very easily be misused. One must stay close to the Lord, in love and obedience, in order to operate in them. Much condemnation and guilt have been laid upon the church when people operate out of the flesh, in suspicion, or natural judgment.

It is one thing to have faith, but as with all the gifts, we as Christians must not to be blind nor ignorant in judging their operation. Just as we are to weigh preaching and check out the preached word with what Scripture says, so we must know the Scriptures to enable us to better understand, receive or reject and judge when the gifts are operating. Don't be overly suspicious or you may miss a blessing, but at the same time learn to eat the good meat of ministry and spit out the bones.

First Corinthians 13 says that we prophesy in part, and I believe that is true with all the gifts. We as channels are not perfect even though the gifts come perfect from God. That is why we must judge ministry by the word of God.

Chapter Eight

The Power Gifts

What drew people to Jesus? Of course, his compassion, his grace-filled words about a loving God who wanted to be their "abba," their daddy; His identification with the common people.

But there were many itinerant preachers who undoubtedly had stirring messages. What set Jesus apart from the others, what compelled people to listen to Him was at least in part the signs and wonders that announced and confirmed what He taught. Signs and wonders proved that God had sent Him.

When we talk about signs and wonders today, for the most part, we are thinking about the power gifts—the gift of healing, the gift of miracles, and their companion gift, faith.

The gift of faith

Several years ago as I was in prayer, the Lord dropped into

my innermost being the gift of faith for the healing of a dear friend, Shade. She had been diagnosed as having several growths in her colon that needed to be surgically removed. There was a possibility that they could be malignant. As I prayed, a supernatural faith rose up inside me that was not my everyday faith. I didn't want to be presumptuous so I prayed and even let time lapse before I called Shade on the phone and told her I believed God was going to heal her and she would not need surgery. Her doctor, who was a Christian, gave her one month to seek God's supernatural healing apart from surgery. Daily I encouraged Shade through praying with her, sharing scriptures from the Bible, and through other gifts of the Spirit, such as the word of knowledge, wisdom, and prophecy as God directed me. Many others were praying for her also. At the end of the month she returned to the doctor's office for further tests, but he found that every growth had completely disappeared. This did not surprise me as all along I had the assurance of her healing because God supernaturally dropped into me that gift of faith. The growths have never returned in the 24 years that have passed since then.

We cannot muster up the gift of faith. It is a gift, which means God sovereignly drops it into our hearts to accomplish a work that He wishes to see done.

Another example

Judy received a call from her daughter telling her that her three-year-old granddaughter, Susan, had a debilitating disease that was causing the child much pain and weakness. Susan could no longer squat without falling over or climb stairs. The doctors so far had been unable to diagnose the disease. The news threw Susan into a dark depression, from which there seemed no way out. The only prayer she could pray for the next three days was "Help!" On the third day God supernaturally dropped the gift of faith into Judy's heart—faith that Susan would be healed. With that faith came supernatural joy as well.

"I just knew Susie was going to be okay," Judy relates. "Even though tests got lost and it took another six months before the disease was diagnosed as an auto-immune condition in which the body digests its own protein, though doctors could not agree on the treatment, I didn't have a moment of fear or disbelief. I could pray and praise the Lord because I *knew* Sue was going to get well."

Sue did get well. Today at 18, she is not only a strong and healthy young woman who shows no signs of the disease, she is a top athlete in a variety of sports.

In 1 Corinthians 12:11 we read that the gifts operate as the Spirit wills, not as we will. After the work God desires to accomplish is done, He removes the gift of faith from us until He desires to give it again. In other words, none of us walk continually in this tremendously powerful realm of faith. We must be open to the Spirit and be willing to be a channel of the gifts but we can't turn the gifts on and off as we will.

Natural faith — saving faith — faith, the fruit

There are three others kinds of faith. One is natural faith. Everyone has faith in something. I have faith in God; many people have faith in their own abilities. The demons have faith in Jesus because they know Him, but their faith only causes them to tremble. Faith that doesn't change a life is sadly lacking.

A higher step of faith is saving faith: *"Believe in the Lord Jesus Christ and you will be saved"* (Acts 16:31). Many people stop at this level of faith and miss out on much of their inheritance as Christians. They may be born again but miss out on the joy of letting Jesus guide their lives.

The third kind of faith is the fruit of faith or faithfulness (Gal. 5:22). Like all fruit, this kind of faith grows with time and nourishment. As we study the word of God, mature as Christians, and let the Spirit guide our lives, the fruit of faith increases.

You can see that the gift of faith is far more powerful than any other kind. We must desire this kind of faith (1 Cor. 14:1) and exercise it by stepping out boldly but humbly as the Spirit leads us. When special demands are made upon us, we can go forth confidently, knowing God will give us the special faith needed to enable us to fulfill His purposes.

The gift of healing

The gift of healing refers to many and diversified healings. It is the divine ability to impart healing to a person who is sick, injured, or handicapped. It is the compassion and power of Jesus working through a human to meet physical or mental needs without natural means. Healing which takes place instantaneously, can be considered a miracle. Most healings come gradually over a period of time.

There are many ways to be healed that are not the gift of healing. One is by the Word of God. *"He sent forth his word and healed them"* (Ps. 107:20). Another is by prayer and belief. *"Whatever you ask for in prayer, believe that you have received it, and it will be yours"* (Mark 11:24). Another way we receive healing is as we pray the prayer of faith, lay hands on the sick and/or anoint them with oil. *"Is there any of you sick? He should call the elders of the church to pray over him and anoint him with oil in the name of the Lord. And the prayer offered in faith will make the sick person well "* (Jas. 5:14-15).

The gift of healing in action

Jesus and the disciples ministered powerfully in the gift of healing. Some have estimated that 90 percent of Jesus' recorded ministry on earth involved healing. Matthew alone records the healing of a leper (8:2-4); a centurion's servant (8:5-13); Peter's mother-in-law (8:14); several demon-possessed people (12:22-23, 15:22-28, 17:14-17); a paralyzed boy (9:2-7); a woman who had been hemorrhaging for 12 years (9:19-20); two blind men (20:30-34) as well as many instances when Jesus healed entire crowds of people who thronged about him everywhere He went.

Another example of the gift of healing is recorded in Acts 9:33-34. Peter walked into the room of Aeneas who had been an invalid for eight years and told him, *'Jesus Christ heals you. Get up and take care of your mat. Immediately Aeneas got up."* This was the gift of healing in action.

Peter could not just walk into any sick person's bedroom and heal him. He had to be led by the Spirit of God. Peter had to have a close enough relationship with God to know the difference between when he wanted someone healed and when the Spirit was moving through him to bring the gift of healing.

Shortly after Kay and her mother Florence were baptized in the Holy Spirit, they visited Kay's grandmother, Grace, who had cataracts on both her eyes. The night before they left, believing they were in the Lord's will, they prayed that Grace's eyes would be healed. When they finished praying, Grace looked out the window, and seeing a street light across the street, remarked, "That light is certainly bright tonight." A week later, she called Florence. Crying with happiness, she related that when she returned to her doctor for a checkup, he told her, with some amazement, that her cataracts were gone.

How can we know when the Spirit wants to bring a gift of

healing through us? Don't expect to be 100 percent right at first. I have found that a compassion rises within me towards the sick person when God wants to use me as a channel of His gifts. I have a natural sympathy for the sick but when this powerful compassion comes and stays with me I really pray and seek God for further direction. The compassion tells me that God wants me involved in a particular case. I visualize a gift all wrapped in pretty paper and a bow and I then just deliver it. When you think of being the delivery person and not the one who had to buy the gift, the pressure is off. Just deliver God's gift and rejoice as the recipient unwraps the gift. Enjoy it with them.

The working of miracles

The gift of miracles is the God-given ability to do supernatural acts. Just as there are many kinds of faith, there are many kinds of miracles. Is there a Christian alive today who hasn't experienced God's miracles? I know the Lord has performed miracles in my life. Fifteen years ago, He spoke to us about a new house on our vacant lot, but financially, building one was impossible. In fact, we even sold the lot. A builder started to build and my spirit said, "He's building it for you!" Impossible? No! God performed many miracles to make it possible for us to buy our new home. We had to act and wait, but we raised five children in that much bigger house we wanted and needed so desperately. As wonderful as my miracle was it was not the gift of miracles. The gift of miracles described in the Bible are the powerful supernatural miracles Jesus performed, such as

1. Turning water into wine (John 2:11)

2. Causing the storm to cease (Mark 6:45-52).

3. The raising of Lazarus and the widow's son (John 11:1-44, Luke 7:11-15)

4. The feeding of the multitudes (Luke 9:10-17)

5. The healing of the centurion's servant (Luke 7: 1-10).

The gift of miracles today

While many of us may never see the gift of miracles in operation today, evangelists on the front line report miracles that occur on their crusades. Most of these fall under the category of miracles of healing. Evangelists Rod and Trena McDougal recently ministered in Romania where they saw a blind girl healed; people getting out of their wheelchairs; a paralyzed elderly man, a six-year-old boy and a 20-year-old woman all restored to health; a deaf girl's hearing restored as well as many more healings.

I believe as the days grow darker, we will begin to see more miracles. We as Christians walk with a miracle-working God. I believe God is very pleased when we expect miracles. We never deserve the grace of God but He is a grace-giving, merciful God. We can expect miracles because God is a good God and desires to love us and others through us as we bring miracles to the hurting world.

Chapter Nine

The Gifts —
a Demonstration
of the Gospel

The aroma filtered down the aisle in the grocery store. As I wheeled my cart toward the meat counter, the smell was unmistakably that of cooking sausage. My mouth watered as I came closer and closer to the demonstration stand. A petite, motherly lady handed me a small bite of the delicious sizzling sausage on a bright green toothpick.

"We have a special today," she said. Her lacy, white apron over a pink and blue cotton dress reminded me of mother and home cooking.

I put that tiny bite of sausage in my mouth. "Slightly salty," I thought, but the hickory-smoke flavor created a desire for more, much more. The only question in my mind was whether to buy three or four packages of the sausage. I decided on four as my freezer would hold whatever I couldn't use right away.

I continued down the aisle. I saw many other specials: two for the price of one, a green tag special, a yellow tag special. Yet I bought few of these. Why? What convinced me that the sausage was a bargain I could not pass by? The *demonstration* of it; no long speech on its virtues, but tasting the real thing for myself. I was convinced through participation. When it comes to food, eating is the best way of proving if what is said about it is really true.

A Christian parallel

There is parallel here for the Christian life.

Recently, my friend, Marge, shared an experience she'd had while attending a retreat. She said she was sitting in a crowded retreat workshop thinking how much she wanted to know that God really loved *her*, Marge. While that thought was still in her mind, the lady sitting behind her put her hand on Marge's shoulder and said, "I don't know why, but I feel like Jesus wants me to tell you that He dearly loves you." Tears trickled down Marge's cheeks as she felt the personal touch of God's love. God really cared so much about her that He miraculously moved a lady to deliver the exact words she longed to hear.

Marge's whole being responded to God as the worship continued. "Jesus, you really do love me, don't you?"

The testimony reminds me of the sausage on the bright green toothpick. What God did may be a small thing, but it proved that He was real. He demonstrated His reality through an obedient, available sister.

The gospel demonstrated by Jesus and Paul

Jesus demonstrated the gospel. He not only preached, He healed the sick. He performed mighty miracles, He even raised the dead. Acts 1:1 says that Jesus began *"to do and teach."* Notice, He *began* the work, but we are to finish it. Scripture says that after Jesus ascended into heaven, *"They* (the disciples) *went forth and preached everywhere, the Lord working with them, and confirming the Word by the signs that followed"* (Mark 16:20 ASV).

The "do" or demonstration of the gospel is to make the spiritual taste buds function. The demonstration gets people's attention so they will listen with faith to the preaching. This was exactly my friend Marge's experience as the spiritual gift of a "word of knowledge" was given to her by the stranger.

The world has a right to expect Christians to demonstrate the gospel. Paul says in Romans 15:19 that the gospel was not fully preached until there was a demonstration of it. He also says that he came not preaching with enticing words of man's wisdom but with *"only a demonstration of the power of the Spirit'* (1 Cor. 2:4-5 TJB).

Jesus demonstrated the gospel by yielding to the will of His father and allowing the Holy Spirit to work through Him—as He healed the leper (Matt. 8:4), as He imparted a portion of His Father's knowledge (the word of knowledge) to the Samaritan woman, telling her that she had five husbands (John 4:18). The gift of miracles was operating through Him as He fed the five thousand (John 6:9-13). We could go on and on and see that the demonstration of the gospel by Jesus was through the same empowering of the Spirit that is available to us. By using the gifts of the Spirit we do the works of God.

We are told that these gifts are to continue until Jesus comes again. *"So that you come behind in no gift, waiting for the coming of our Lord Jesus Christ."* (1 Cor. 1:7).

Paul tells us in First Corinthians 12:1 that we must not be ignorant of the gifts. It seems someone is trying to keep Christians ignorant of them. Do you suppose his name is Satan and he hates people smelling the aroma and taking a bite? Would he rather we not demonstrate the gospel?

Years ago as a young Christian I was told that the gifts of the Spirit were no longer operating in the Body of Christ. When Russ and I went to the mission field to spread the gospel, we didn't know that the nine gifts of the Holy Spirit were available for us. We did the best we could but we were very disappointed that we didn't see the power of God in our ministry. I might still be ignorant about the gifts except since then I've seen and experienced them so many times that I couldn't doubt if I tried.

Personal experiences

Two personal experiences come to mind. Some time ago I was having trouble breathing deeply. I could only take short breaths. When I breathed deeply, the pain shot through my lungs and back. I probably had a virus or maybe even pleurisy, but I felt it would go away sooner or later. However, the days and weeks went on and the pain was still there.

Then one night at a church service, someone in the congregation started to sing, "Reach Out and Touch the Lord," and we all joined in. The song leader had us repeat the song but this time he suggested we really reach out to Jesus in faith for any need we had and Jesus would touch us. In simple faith I did as he suggested and asked Jesus to heal my virus or pleurisy or whatever it was. I didn't feel anything at the moment but the next day I noticed I could breathe deeply without any pain. This was my first experience of healing.

The second involved a chronic lower back pain I had. As a young girl, I had been able to lift almost anything without its affecting my back. But a few years ago I found that whenever

I lifted a heavy object, I would suffer severe pain. One day while driving to a prayer meeting, I was experiencing such a pain. I had overlifted again; the pain was the result. I sat through the meeting with difficulty. But I was soon to get some heavenly relief.

As the offering was being taken, the music leader went to the microphone and announced that God was healing people in the congregation with back problems. He said to accept *our* healing as we sang the words of the next song.

Our voices rang out, "Savior, Savior, hear my humble cry. While on others thou are falling, do not pass me by." Racing through my mind was "How do I accept? How do I get Jesus to touch me and not pass *me* by?" I found myself in a half-panic state, afraid I was going to miss out. Suddenly, I had to laugh at myself. "Lord, forgive me," I prayed. "I admit I don't really know how to receive but I trust you right now." I knew His nature was a giving one. I relaxed and enjoyed the rest of the meeting, forgetting about my back. As I was driving home I suddenly noticed I had no pain. I twisted and turned as much as I could in my seat belt and still, there was no pain. The Lord had really touched me. "I'm healed! I'm healed!" I cried.

What happened?

Let's take a look at what happened. The song leader had been given the word of knowledge that God was healing backs, and he had stepped out in faith and announced it. Faith was also created in the hearts of those who needed healing, and there were healings, and possibly miracles, in the form of instant healing. On that occasion I had probably received the gift of faith as well as a miracle. At least four gifts of God were released in a few seconds as the Holy Spirit moved across the congregation and healed backs. All this happened while people were passing the offering plates. I will always be amazed at how low-keyed God frequently is. No fanfare. After the last plate was brought forward and a prayer given to bless the offering, the meeting continued. Only God knows how many people were healed in those few minutes. **The gospel was demonstrated to us personally.** Nothing was visible to others about my healing but I have never forgotten that moment many years ago. Jesus confirmed His word by healing my back. The sign that followed the word of knowledge was that I had no more pain. Hallelujah!

I am reminded of another experience, one involving prophecy. I had taken my very discouraged friend and neighbor to her first meeting at a church where the gifts of the Spirit were openly encouraged. She was going through a divorce and had also discovered she was three months pregnant at age 42. Someone gave a prophecy which described my friend's condition. The prophecy was directed to a daughter with a heavy burden, who felt rejected and was in a situation that seemed unbearable. God told her in the prophecy that He would take care of her and that she was safe in His hands. My friend wept with joy as she received that prophecy by faith for herself and her unborn child.

The child is now a beautiful, happy, eight-year-old. I've watched through the years as God has faithfully cared for this little family. The child has been her mother's greatest blessing in all this time.

God's words, through prophecy, gave her peace and courage to live one day at a time.

The gifts bless us

As we have seen, the gifts of God are a real blessing to those in need. I know of many, more spectacular healings, such as that of a cancer patient in Victoria, British Columbia, who was cured or the case of a lady in Spokane, Washington, whose rheumatoid arthritis completely disappeared half an hour after prayer. In the latter instance, the woman admits she really didn't believe God would heal her and yet God in His mercy touched her and set her free.

Numbers 14:21 says, *"But as truly as I live, all the earth shall be filled with the glory of the Lord."* The glory of the Lord is the manifest presence of God; in other words, how God manifests Himself or proves His Word to us. This promise was given to Moses and I believe it is being fulfilled in our day. God is moving and revealing His glory through yielded vessels. As Christians, we have the challenge before us to release God's glory and fulfill the words in Numbers.

Our responsibility is to get over our "ignorance" of spiritual gifts, be available as a channel of the Holy Spirit to be used by Him as He wills, to demonstrate the gospel and leave the results, however small or big, in His hands.

Chapter Ten

Co-laboring with God

The phone rang and on the other end of the line was Barbara, one of my precious sisters in the Lord. "Fran, you have just got to help me!" she cried. "My brother, Tom, is a homosexual but he wants to be set free. He loves the Lord, and he used to be a church soloist. But when he asked his pastor and several other Christian men for help, they told him he can't possibly be a Christian and still have this problem. He's so desperate he's almost ready to give up and accept his problem as a condition he got into because of sin. He's afraid he'll have to live this way the rest of his life."

My heart went out to this young man. Jesus came to set man free. He doesn't want anyone to be a captive. I quickly prayed and felt I was to minister to Tom.

Ministering to Tom

It is always good to minister in twos or more. I called my

prayer partner, Shade, and the Lord showed her she should minister with me. When Shade and I and Barbara and Tom got together and began to pray, the Lord gave a word of prophecy that changed Tom's life. God told him in the prophecy that he was accepted and loved by God, that God was pleased because Tom was seeking Him with his whole heart, and He promised Tom that he indeed would be set free to love, worship, and serve God again. As that beautiful word came forth, Tom raised his hands and face to God. Then with the prophecy the Holy Spirit gave a word of knowledge: "My son, you have often looked in the mirror and cursed yourself for being a homosexual." This word really got to Tom as he knew the one prophesying could not possibly know this on her own. He also realized that God did not overlook his deep self-hatred. God went on to tell him he was a precious son of God and could be set free. Immediately another word of knowledge came saying that God the Holy Spirit was upon him right then and if he opened his mouth, he could speak in tongues and offer that praise to God that had been cut off so long by his sin. It was beautiful to watch him begin to speak in tongues and praise God. We all sang in tongues and rejoiced as God began to deliver His precious son. What hours of counseling could not do, God did in 15 minutes. The following week Tom took communion for the first time in years. He was set free, knowing no sin is too great to be forgiven. He is now meeting with us periodically for strength and encouragement. What a student of the Word he is becoming, and the Word will give him the strength to live in his times of temptation. He can now go to church and receive from God with a free spirit and a clear conscience as an equal with others sitting around him.

I love to co-labor with God!

God wants co-laborers

From the beginning of time, God has invited us to be His co-laborers. In Second Corinthians God calls us His fellow workers (8:23), and Mark tell us: *"Then the disciples went out and preached everywhere, and the Lord worked with them and confirmed his word by the signs that accompanies it"* (Mark 16:20). In other words, the Lord worked – co-labored with the disciples and He does the same with us. We lay hands on the sick and God heals them. We tell someone about Jesus' sacrifice and the Lord changes their hearts. We do the natural, but God does the supernatural. Aren't you glad it's not the other way around?

God has a plan for this earth and as we co-labor with Him, the following scriptures should inspire us:

1. *"The earth will be filled with the knowledge of the glory of the Lord, as the waters cover the sea"* (Hab. 2:14)

2. *"I am going to do something in your days that you would not believe even if you were told"* (Hab. 1:5)

3. *"Don't you know that you yourselves are God's temple and that God's spirit lives in you?"* (1 Cor. 3:16).

4. *"And we, who with unveiled faces all reflect the Lord's glory, are being transformed into his likeness with ever-increasing glory, which comes from the Lord, who is the Spirit"* (2 Cor. 3:7).

We are anointed

Where do we get the power to be co-laborers with God? From Jesus, "the anointed one," who lives in us. Look at what Scripture has to say about the anointing of Jesus and of us.

Speaking of Himself, Jesus said, *"The Spirit of the Lord is on me, because he has anointed me" (Luke 4:18).*

"He anointed us" (2 Cor. 2:21).

"You have an anointing from the Holy One" (1 John 2:20).

"As for you, the anointing you received from Him remains in you" (1 John 2:27.)

Stirring up the anointing

Because the Holy Spirit lives in us, we know we always have an anointing. We don't have to fast and pray before we dare to step out and co-labor with God. God continually stirs up our anointing as we ask Him. In my morning devotional time I remind God that His anointing is in me and I ask Him to stir it up for the day's tasks that lie ahead, to enable me to do what I need to do. Today I plan to write. I need a fresh stirring up. I ask God and my writing is easier, the thoughts come with less effort. It's fun to write. I also know I may get phone calls from people requesting prayer or counseling. Today I pray that I might give Jesus-life to those in need. To be a good wife and mother I need God's stirring up and when I speak or teach even though I may have taught the material many times.

The Results of the anointing

Everything Jesus did, He did under the anointing of God the Holy Spirit. God anointed Jesus *"to preach the good news to the poor....to proclaim freedom for the prisoners and recovery of sight for the blind, to release the oppressed, to proclaim the year of the Lord's favor"* (Luke 4:18-19) or if you prefer the original passage from Isaiah *"to preach good news to the poor....to bind up the brokenhearted, to proclaim freedom for the captives and release from darkness for the prisoners, to proclaim the year of the Lord's favor"* (Isa. 61:1-2). Acts 10:38 tells us *"God anointed Jesus with the Holy Spirit and power."* Jesus and God co-labored and things happened. Jesus was not independent. He depended on His Father's anointing. We too must depend on God's anointing.

In Psalm 92:10 we read, *"Fine oils have been poured upon me."*

Oil is a symbol for the anointing. See the results of the anointing given in the following verses.

1. I'll see my enemies defeated (vv. 11-12).

2. I'll be like a palm tree able to bend and not break in the storms of life (v. 12).

3. I'll grow strong in the Lord (v. 12). A cedar of Lebanon is a very strong tree.

4. I'll be planted in God's house where I'll flourish (no more roller coaster rides) (v. 13).

5. I'll be an effective co-laborer with God even when I am old (v. 14).

6. I'll stay fresh and green, growing, on fire in my relationship with God until the moment I die (v. 14).

Corporate anointing

I believe God is anointing His Body with new power. Corporate anointing happens to the Body of Christ at times. Second Chronicles 5:11-14 tells us about the 120 priests who had consecrated themselves to the Lord and were praising God. "They *couldn't stand because of the presence of the Lord (the anointing)."* They were all slain in the Spirit. We are seeing this today in many meetings as God displays His presence. Laughter and joy often break out on the congregation when the Lord is present.

Scripture teaches us that the joy of the Lord is our strength. The Body of Christ desperately needs more joy and strength. When God sends holy laughter on a group, His joy brings a supernatural strength along with it. The corporate anointing I see today is an anointing of joy and healing. As people are slain in the Spirit, God heals them physically and emotionally. God does a quick work when the corporate anointing falls upon a congregation.

Letting Jesus lead

To co-labor with God is to follow His leading. It means we move with the glory cloud, the anointing (See Exodus 40:36-37). Many Christians miss a new move of God because they refuse to move on when God wants them to. Many Christians missed what God did during the charismatic renewal because they had their own agenda and they camped there while God was moving on to new groups.

God is moving to bring in the harvest. I see many lay people being stirred by the Holy Spirit to witness on the job, to their friends, relatives, and neighbors. The cloud is moving to bring in the harvest. With that cloud comes special grace from God. The task is easy, fun, and fruitful when we "see" what the Father is doing and co-labor with Him.

Keeping clean — the cross and the blood are for sins

If we are to be successful co-laborers with God, we must continually let the Blood of Jesus wash us of our daily sin. Then and only then will we be a pure vessel for His use. Notice that the following verses imply that we must take action to stay clean by the Blood of Jesus:

1. *"Let us purify ourselves"* (2 Cor. 7:1).

2. *"If a man cleanses himself from the latter (ignoble purposes), he will be an instrument for noble purposes, made holy, useful to the Master and prepared to do any good work"* (2 Tim. 2:21).

3. *"Everyone who has this hope in him (God the Father) purifies himself just as he is pure"* (1 John 3:3).

Motivated by love

As co-laborers with God, we must be motivated by love. As we spend time in the presence of Jesus our needs are met. Our need to be loved and cherished — our need to be of value, not by what we do for God, but by who we are in Him. We then can co-labor with Him from a sense of security and wholeness. He will supply us with His love and His faith to do His work.

Second Corinthians 5:14 says, *"For the love of Christ constrains us."* It's His love working through me that keeps me hanging in there when I am under the enemy's attack. My human love is not enough. It has been said that the key to evangelism is love (John 13:34-35). It took 30 years of loving and prayer before my sister, Linda, accepted Jesus. Love unlocked the rusty lock on the door of her heart. She often tells how much it meant to her that I continued to love her even though she "appeared" to be uninterested in the gospel. I sent her books to read that she never read (She tells me now), but the act of sending her the books spoke love to her. Love must be what motivates us to co-labor with God. If you lack love, ask for it.

Years ago I read these words, "It's better to love than to be right." The Holy Spirit is quick to remind me when these words are to be applied to a particular situation. Our human nature cries out to win, to be right, but love yields, gives a soft answer, and then we really win.

Love's enemy

In our zeal to co-labor with God, we must not become too busy. The other day as I driving in my car and listening to the radio I heard a man say, "Love is spelled t-i-m-e." Wow! I chewed on that statement for several miles. God reminded me of a situation from my childhood. I was living at the Washington Children's Home, having just been released from six weeks of confinement in a youth detention center. I felt so unloved. Several of us were sent to Bible camp where God really began to draw me to Himself. My camp counselor showed me unconditional love. I felt it but because it was hard for me to trust (after living in 13 foster homes), I tested that love to see if it was real. After the week of camp, I returned to the children's home. I wrote the counselor a letter and she answered it. I knew she had 75 new campers but she took the time to answer my letter, not just that one but several during the summer. On the Fourth of July, she and another counselor drove 30 miles to the children's home to take some of us to the fireworks. I knew she was sharing her time with us and that spoke true love into my heart.

Her love was enough to heal me so that when Billy Graham came to Seattle later that summer I received Jesus as my Savior. Words such as, "I love you," may have been easy for her to say, but when she took t-i-m-e, I knew it was love. God's love flowing through her expressed in a way I knew was love. Seeing, feeling that kind of love from one of God's children gave me hope that maybe God too loved me.

Cooperating with the wind of the Spirit

To co-labor with God means to be aware of and to co-operate with the wind of the Spirit. Jesus only did what He saw the Father doing. That is why He was so successful. That is why He never had spiritual burnout or had a stress attack. Ephesians 2:10 tells us that God prepared in advance the good work we are to do. I believe this means that long ago God had my agenda for today planned. It is just right for me, not too much work and not too little, not beyond my ability and yet challenging. I need His presence, His anointing to do the work He has prepared in advance for me to do. Then I can truly be the kind of co-laborer the Lord is seeking.

Chapter Eleven

Learning to Minister in the Gifts

God is no respecter of persons. He wants all of us to minister in the gifts of the Holy Spirit, to use those supernatural abilities He imparts to us for the good of others and as proof of who He is. Just as He gave me the ability to minister, He will do the same for you. Perhaps my experiences will help and encourage you.

Even though I felt too unworthy for God to use me in the gifts, I still dared to ask Him. He answered that prayer in our small weekly prayer meeting. As we prayed, I began to get encouraging thoughts for the other members. I believed that the messages were inspired by the Holy Spirit so I spoke them out. Often someone would tell me that she was really encouraged by what I had spoken. As I prayed in tongues, more and more thoughts would come. Or I would see a picture and in my inner thoughts I would receive a beautiful encouraging message (word). By faith I would share it. My friends also began to get thoughts, pictures, impressions, or hear the inner voice of God.

One of the members of our group was told she needed surgery to remove several growths that could be malignant, and we began to pray earnestly for her healing. When she went back to her doctor a few weeks later, the growths had miraculously disappeared. We were encouraged to pray more and more for healing. Gertrude Ticer, a woman who had been miraculously healed of muscular dystrophy, shared her exciting testimony with our group. Jesus had come into her hospital room when she was near death and healed her. He also told her to stay in the hospital three more days so that the doctors, nurses, and patients could see what God had done. Many people witnessed this miracle and received Jesus as their personal Savior. One man scheduled for surgery, who knew Gertrude, saw her and said, "If Jesus can heal Gertrude, He can heal me." He canceled the surgery and went home healed.

Our prayer group began to pray fervently for the sick. We experienced many healings but also found that not everyone we prayed for was healed (one person even died). At first, this was very disappointing to us, but we continued to pray for healing anyway. We learned to leave the results in God's hands.

Teaching others what I learned

In 1971 I was asked to teach on the gifts of the Holy Spirit at Jane Hansen's home. Later Jane became Women's Aglow international president. This women's organization was born out of a desire of four women to minister to other women. In 1967 I attended the first luncheon of Aglow held in Seattle,

Washington. Our faith was very limited: we believed God was going to use this organization to minister to women in the Seattle area. God, however, had much bigger plans and today Aglow has chapters in over 100 nations, women ministering to women and reaching families for Christ.

Women's Aglow—a place to minister

I became involved in Women's Aglow by serving on the International Aglow Ministry Board for several years. This involvement opened many doors for me to teach on the gifts of the Holy Spirit. Aglow began to produce Bible studies and I was asked to co-author a study on the gifts. It has since been translated into other languages and is being used around the world. I see this as part of the fulfillment of Sister Woodward's prophecy that I would go around the world teaching on the gifts.

Taping prophetic words

I took my tape recorder everywhere with me because I saw the benefit of having the prophetic word on tape. When someone gave me a prophetic word, I usually was able to tape it. I then transcribed the words given to me. I noticed that many of the words were for the future. I didn't want to forget them so by taping and writing them down I could easily review them. They have been a real faith builder in my life.

I was offered 700 tapes for ten cents each at a fire sale. Seventy dollars was a lot of money to me, but I stepped out in faith and bought the tapes, and God provided the money to pay for them. Opportunities to teach and prophesy continued to open for me. I was invited to speak in churches, retreats, and home prayer meetings. Soon I had used up the 700 tapes. By this time I was so encouraged by those who received a prophetic word on tape, that I decided to trust God and buy another 1,000 tapes. I continue to purchase tapes for this purpose, not for ten cents, but the cost is no longer an issue. I want God's people to be blessed over and over again by His word to them. Taping the prophetic word makes this possible.

Prophesy to everyone?

Early in my ministry days I prophesied to only six or eight people at a meeting because that's how I saw others do it. One evening I ministered to everyone in a home meeting except one man. He was so hurt that he ran out of the house crying. He thought that God had rejected him. I felt terrible and I ran after him to tell him it was my fault, not God's. Soon God showed me that I could minister to everyone if the groups were kept small, so I began limiting the home meetings to groups of 20 people. If you are wondering if ministering to everyone is scriptural, let me share what the Lord showed me. The Bible says we prophesy according to our faith. In the early days of ministry, I didn't have the faith to prophesy to everyone. But faith comes as you step out and exercise the faith you do have. God is more willing to speak through us than we are willing to yield ourselves to Him for His use.

Ongoing process

Learning how to minister in the gifts of the Holy Spirit is an ongoing process. The key is relationship with the Lord. As we grow in this beautiful relationship we learn to hear His voice more clearly. We learn He is a loving, merciful God. As we study and meditate on the Scriptures, faith comes. The more we know God and His word, the more success we will experience in ministry.

Where and how do we begin?

The best place to begin to learn how to prophesy and pray for the needs of others is in a small prayer group. The love and faith shared here will be a compelling ingredient to make you step out and begin. Also, if you make a mistake, the love will encourage you to keep on even though you aren't perfect.

When my friend faced surgery, love for her motivated me to yield to God so He would touch her. I would pray for her and then call her on the phone and prophesy to her. I did this daily for a month. Why? Because of love. One prophecy said she was to wait on God and He would give her three scriptures to stand on in faith. During her prayer time, she felt God give her the three scriptures. She wrote them down and placed them in her kitchen window. When fear overwhelmed her, she read these scriptures. This was a form of spiritual warfare. We anointed her with oil, prayed for her and the result was that she didn't need surgery because God healed her. Praise the Lord!

How we receive

How does one receive a word of prophecy, a word of wisdom or a word of knowledge? 1 Corinthians 14:13 answers that in one word: *pray*. So step one is to ask God to give you the gifts and from then on *faith* is the key. Faith, of course, comes by knowing what God's word is saying, so faith in God's Word and simple trust are prerequisites. Jesus was always moved by compassion before ministering. Before I minister, I ask the Lord to let me feel what He feels. What a key that has been, as invariably compassion, mercy, grace and understanding flood over me, and my ministry becomes one of love and not judgment. Soon words, thoughts or pictures begin to come to mind that I am trusting are from the Lord. In faith I begin to speak out. As I take that step of faith, God honors that, and more and more words begin to come. A beginner may have only one sentence. That is great! God doesn't need a lot of words to get His message across. To me some of the greatest messages of the Bible are in a very few words. For example, notice the powerful message in the following words, *"For God so loved the world that He gave...."* (John 3:16); *"For all have sinned"* (Rom. 3:23); *"In all your ways acknowledge him, and he will make yours paths straight"* (Prov. 3:6).

The Bible is the best source of prophecy, so if the Holy Spirit directs you to quote part of a scripture, know that this is, as we say, "right on." Often the Holy Spirit uses a quoted scripture as a springboard and the prophecy may continue in words not quoted directly from Scripture.

As I was ministering to the young homosexual I mentioned in a previous chapter, I saw him in my mind's eye, under the inspiration of the Holy Spirit, standing before the mirror cursing himself. I also saw the Lord holding his hands and talking face to face with him with tremendous love and compassion. In simple faith, I stepped out and spoke these things. Now the question in many of your hearts may be: how do I know it isn't just me speaking? That bothered me until I heard a cute little song. It goes, "Sugar in the tea, Jesus and me. You can't take the sugar out of the tea and you can't take Jesus out of me." So I simply believe Jesus can't help but come through.

How to prophesy

Here are a few suggestions I have learned along the way to help you minister in the gift of prophecy.

1. Be free in your prayer language. Speak in tongues for a few seconds, and while you are speaking in tongues God may give you thoughts, pictures, or a scripture.

Give what you have and wait on Him for more.

2. Know that God wants you to prophesy: "*You may all prophesy,*" (1 Cor. 14:31).

3. Simple faith releases the flow. "*If a man's gift is prophesying let him use it in proportion to his faith*" (Rom. 12:6).

4. Relax, don't get emotional. Keep it brief. You are in control. (1 Cor. 14:31).

5. Start now and speak what God gives you. Begin! Begin! Begin!

The harvest

The harvest is plentiful. God is looking for those who will labor to bring in that harvest. His way has always been through the demonstration of His love and power that is available through the gifts of the Holy Spirit—human initiative and divine sovereignty.

Chapter Twelve

Satan's Tactics to Keep You from Ministering

Spencer, my five-year-old grandson, has learned how to print his name. He gets all the letters down on paper but not always on the same line. If he runs out of space he puts the "left over" letters anywhere that is available on the paper. I don't criticize him but I encourage him because I know encouragement will help him grow. He is so happy when he hears Grandma say, "Well done, Spencer. You are doing such a good job, and I'm so proud of you." I am sometimes tempted to say, "Well done, Spencer, but . . . " However, I've learned through experience that the "buts" are very discouraging, especially to a beginner.

God has work for each one of us to do. The gifts of the Holy Spirit are our tools to do that work. Ephesians 4:12 says the gifts are *"to prepare God's people for works of service, so that the body of Christ may be built up."* The work of those in ministry is to build up the body so each can do his work. Lay people often expect the pastor to do all the ministry. Pastors need to teach the lay people how to minister, to pick them up when they fall, and to encourage them to keep going.

The key words in Ephesians are *"to prepare God's people."* How are God's people prepared? By encouragement! Spencer, my grandson, will grow in printing his name. Right now it would be unfair to compare his printing to that of his six-year-old cousin who has a year of first grade behind him and has already been taught the "How to's of printing." Spencer needs to hear words of approval to motivate him to go on.

Just as we have a God who wants to encourage us, we have an enemy, Satan, who will do anything to discourage us and keep us from ministering in the gifts. Let's look at a few of his strategies.

Insensitivity—a weapon of the enemy

The church was filled with over a thousand people worshipping God in song. A few brave ones were dancing. The air was filled with excitement and joy. The pastor invited anyone who had a word from the Lord to come up to the microphone. A lady I knew slightly went forward to give a prophetic word. I was sitting in the balcony and I watched her as she waved her arms in praise to God. Caught up in the joy of His presence, she moved her feet slightly in an impromptu dance. I knew it was not easy for her to go up to that microphone and speak.

Suddenly, the pastor turned to her and said, "Lady, sit down and get control of yourself."

I couldn't believe what I was hearing. The church became very still. All eyes were on this very embarrassed woman. She headed back toward her seat but instead of stopping there, she continued out the back door.

The Lord prompted me to go after her. We met in the church foyer. She was in tears. "Fran, what did I do wrong?" she asked. "I'm so confused. I thought I was obeying the Lord. It took a lot of courage for me to walk up in front of all those people but I didn't want to disobey God." I tried to comfort her. After a few minutes she stopped crying and asked what she should do. I suggested she return to her seat. I explained that many people there would be relieved to see her back. The pastor had not shown compassion; in fact, he had quenched and grieved the Spirit. She did go back to her seat for the rest of the service, but I never saw her again.

Leaders need to be very sensitive to the feelings of those who bring a word of prophecy or any other type of ministry. Yes, they must correct but I believe this is a chance to "Do unto others as you would have them do unto you." Wise dads and moms correct their children in private, not in front of the whole neighborhood. If you or anyone you know has been publicly embarrassed as this woman was, don't let the enemy win. His plan is to get you to stop ministering in the power—the gifts of the Holy Spirit. He is threatened by the gifts because they expose his works. Recognize what the enemy has planned and thwart those plans by forgiving those who hurt you. Get back up and keep moving.

Where are they now?

I have observed that many Christians who were once moving in the gifts are no longer growing in this area. I know several people who no longer speak in tongues. "I don't need it any more," one woman told me. "Tongues is useful when you first become a Christian—when you're a baby, really. After all, the Bible calls it 'the least of the gifts.'" I've heard that last statement from several Christians who otherwise know their

Bibles fairly well. Nowhere in Scripture is tongues called "the least of the gifts." This is one of Satan's lies. As for no longer needing a special, intimate language with which we can communicate with God, how can anyone believe that we outgrow it? The longer I move in the gifts, the more I want to be like Paul and "speak in tongues more than any of you."

During the early days of the charismatic renewal there were many teachings on the gifts. Prayer groups sprang up all over the country where these gifts were operating. The Holy Spirit moved greatly in churches and home prayer meetings where the gifts were functioning. Healing, deliverance, encouragement through the prophetic word during these meetings drew many to the Lord. Signs and wonders revealed that God is still present and loves His people.

I was in several prayer groups during those early years of the charismatic movement. We were from a variety of denominational backgrounds and many of us were not being taught about the gifts in our own churches. But when we met for prayer, Bible study, and fellowship we would practice what we were taught by tapes or visiting teachers. If anyone was sick, we prayed for him by anointing with oil and laying on of hands. Miracles happened; prophetic words encouraged.

We all came to the meetings eager to share what God had done for us the previous week. Betty, a vivacious member of one group I was in, came bubbling into a meeting. She and her husband Bob had wanted to go to a large Christian conference held near Seattle each summer. Unfortunately, Bob had lost his job and they had only a small part of the down payment. Believing that God was going to provide a way for them to go, they packed their bags, but when the departure day arrived, they still needed $100. Bob packed the car and they sat around the kitchen table, praying for the money and waiting. At 11:00 a.m., Bob brought in the mail. It included a letter from his elderly aunts, plus a $100 check. Never before had the women sent any money. How we rejoiced with Betty!

Betty and her family lived on small miracles. Another time when they had no money their 14-year-old daughter, Stacey, stepped on a wire in a cow barn with her bare foot. The puncture wound was red and swollen, and a few hours later, although they had soaked her foot and prayed, a red line ran from the foot to her knee. They continued to pray because they didn't even have the money for a tetanus shot. If Jesus didn't heal Stacey, they were in big trouble. As they prayed and went about the evening's activities, the red line started down and by morning they couldn't even find the puncture wound.

False teaching

Last week I called a friend whom I hadn't seen for several years. She had been greatly used by God in the spiritual gifts and we had written a Bible study together on the gifts many years ago. As we talked, she shared how she had backed away from all we had learned. I asked, "How could you back away?" She went on to tell how her church had gone into error. I knew what she was talking about because we had been members of the same church, but we had left and prayer set us free from the enemy's attack and the satanic teaching that was being given there. She and her husband remained for several years longer. By the time they left, they were so disillusioned, they wanted no part of the gifts or speaking in tongues.

When we accept false or erroneous teaching, it is partly our fault. We are not to accept all teaching blindly but to compare it to what the Bible says. If the teaching is wrong, we should gently confront the one teaching. If he will not be corrected, then it is our responsibility to go elsewhere.

'Idolizing' well-known Christians

Sometimes we become so attached to celebrity Christians, it almost becomes a form of idolatry. Many people sit at home on Sunday mornings with their TV preachers instead of going to church. Then when the "idols" let them down, they become disillusioned. A few years back Christians around the world were scandalized when several well known TV evangelists fell from grace. Who will ever know how many judged the entire charismatic movement by the behavior of a few leaders, deciding they didn't want any part of their teachings, including the gifts?

We are always wrong when we look at people, rather than to the giver of the gifts—Jesus Christ. If you are disappointed in someone you formerly respected, don't give Satan another victory. Get your eyes back on Jesus. People will always let us down. Jesus alone will never disappoint us.

Tradition — denominationalism

Another friend who was instrumental in my involvement in the gifts of the Spirit said she had to keep quiet about speaking in tongues and the power of God because the mission board she was working under was against it. So she pulled out. She stopped growing in the use of the gifts because of fear of man. God wants to empower His people but tradition, man-made rules, hinder many from going on.

Harsh judging of gifts

Early in ministry I heard a Bible teacher say, "Judging can be wrong, so stay sweet. Judging can be right, so be adjustable."

I understood this to mean that those in authority who have the responsibility to judge your prophecy or ministry can be wrong in the *way* they judge you. But your responsibility is to stay sweet, teachable, have a right attitude and be willing to forgive. But wait! Their judging can also be right so be teachable, humble, and learn from the experience even though it may be painful. The one judging may be wrong in some aspect while right in others. Pray and ask God to show you the truth and obey what He says. He is the redeemer and will redeem anything we give to Him. What the enemy means for evil, God will bring good out of if we humble ourselves before Him.

Pride

I think my mistakes in ministry have been my best teachers. Making a mistake is painful but if we learn from those mistakes we can still win. If we humble ourselves before God and others, our mistakes can be redeemed. Let me give you an example from my own life.

Over 300 women came to a retreat to hear Bible teaching, experience the gifts of the Spirit in operation, and to praise and worship God in a freedom greater than they had in their own churches. I knew their expectations because I had invited some of them.

The speaker was a well known Bible teacher. Her teaching was excellent but very lengthy, and many left before the teaching was over. Those who stayed to the end were exhausted and immediately headed for their beds. The women had come to the retreat to see and hear the Holy Spirit move through the gifts, but the retreat was so planned and structured that there was no room for the Holy Spirit to move. Several women came to me and complained. I felt a responsibility to please them, but because I wasn't in leadership at this retreat I didn't have authority to change things. One evening, however, I saw a tiny opening and I used it. I delivered a prophetic word and I could tell that many were blessed. While I had the microphone I invited others to give a word. Several responded and although one message brought during those few moments was not biblically correct, I felt my mission was accomplished.

Several days later I received a phone call from the leader of the retreat. She said, "Fran, the devil really used you." I asked how and she said it was my fault that the unscriptural word had been given, because I had encouraged the women to bring words from the Lord. Now being accused of allowing the devil to use me was going for the jugular. I became very defensive. I shared the phone call with my friends and my prayer group. Of course, they all took "my side." We decided to have a meeting with the retreat leadership and clear my record. The day for the meeting came and my friends backed out, and instead of going to the meeting, I went to a pastor for advice. After hearing my story, he said God was after something in me and he gently told me that I had usurped authority that was not mine. He went on to say that I wanted to show the board where they were wrong, but this was the Holy Spirit's responsibility. Instead of defending myself, I needed to repent for my mistake. When I prayed about it, I knew he was right. I wrote a letter of apology for my actions to the leadership and asked their forgiveness. That experience taught me what was meant by, "Judging can be wrong, so stay sweet. Judging can be right so be adjustable."

I needed to be sweet and I also needed to be adjusted. I believe God put me through that test. If I had failed to respond to His way, I could have sabotaged my ministry.

Don't be discouraged by your mistakes. We all make them. Let God use them to teach, not the devil to destroy.

Good works God has prepared

Our greatest joy in this life is when we are fulfilling God's purpose for our life. Ephesians 2:10 says we were created in Christ Jesus *"to do good works which God prepared in advance for us to do."* He has already created those good works for us. We need His ability, His tools, to accomplish these works. Jesus only did what He saw the Father doing. That is why He had such success. He was so in touch with the Father that everything He did produced life. He only did the good works which God prepared in advance for Him to do. But He did them God's way through the gifts of the Holy Spirit. He depended on the Holy Spirit to lead Him and work through Him to do the impossible.

It is through a personal relationship with the Lord that we can know the "good works He has prepared" for each of us to do. As we grow in knowing Him and discern His voice we will also grow in the use of His gifts. We can see tremendous needs in the world. We can get so busy doing good works of various kinds, that we don't have time for anything else. God wants us to know His plan for our lives and to do only what He has prepared in advance for us to do.

Spiritual burnout

Jesus says, "My yoke is easy, my burden is light." After speaking at a retreat and praying for people for hours I was exhausted. I picked up my purse and headed for my room. I was about to leave the big auditorium when a shy young woman who had been afraid to come for prayer earlier tapped me on the shoulder and asked me if I had time to pray for her. I felt anger rise up inside me, but I smiled and said that I did. After I finally got to my room, I had a little argument with the

Lord. "Lord, you said your yoke is easy, your burden light. Why am I so exhausted?" I fell asleep before I heard the Lord's answer, but as time went on, I learned how to avoid burnout. Here are a few tips I'll pass on to you.

1. God wants a personal relationship with us more than our "works." By spending time getting to know Him, loving and praising Him and letting Him love us, we avoid burnout. He will give us our daily instructions for the good works and the burden will be light.

2. I have learned to teach others to minister and to teach people to go to Jesus in those people. The same Jesus that is in me is also in a young Christian.

3. I have learned to say "No" to invitations to speak when my schedule becomes too busy.

4. I have learned to say "No" to other invitations. Just because there is a need, I'm not always God's answer. I've learned to be a referral person. I often get people to contact others who can help them.

5. I've also learned to say "Yes" to just having fun. For ten years I've met monthly with six ladies for fun, fellowship, food, prayer and ministry to each other. That fun and laughter is as important as the ministry time — it is ministry. The joy of the Lord is my strength. After a day with my friends, laughing, joking, and loving one another, I feel strengthened in the Lord.

Satan doesn't want us to minister. He is a crafty adversary and we need to be aware of his strategies and not be taken in or be trapped by them.

Chapter Thirteen

The Spiritual Gifts
in Counseling

"Fran, I've been in counseling for three years and in a support group for two. I feel like I'm stuck. I've learned so much I could be a counselor myself, but I still carry around a lot of pain and garbage. Somehow, I'm missing something. Is there anything else I can do?"

I've heard variations of the above complaint many times. I also hear people say, "I'm going to a Christian counselor but he doesn't really pray with me, or if he does at all, it's only a little prayer at the beginning or end of the session—sort of like tacking God's approval onto the time."

Picking the right counselor

If you need counseling or are considering becoming a counselor, the right kind of counseling is crucial. What is the right kind of counseling? The most effective counselors are those who are totally yielded to the Holy Spirit and have learned to depend on and operate in Him, using the gifts of the Holy Spirit, people who pray in the Spirit and wait on God for direction. Perhaps a word of knowledge will come to them as a key to unlock the pain or bondage suffered by the person in counseling. A word of wisdom will start that person down a path that leads to healing. A word of discernment will reveal when satanic forces are involved.

Many counselors will say they depend on the Holy Spirit, but they also depend on their own understanding or things they've learned. One counselor said the Lord told her to stop reading "Dear Abby" because she was using the syndicated column as a source of much of her counseling.

How different it is with a counselor who operates in the spiritual gifts. My friend, Lorraine, is a busy counselor. Here are a few examples of what happens in her counseling sessions.

Jeanne

As Lorraine began to pray with a counselee, Jeanne, she saw in the Spirit a pair of little baby sandals. Lorraine told Jeanne what she was seeing and asked her, "Does that mean anything to you?"

Jeanne began to cry. When she could speak again, she told Lorraine that when she was a little girl her baby sister, Candy, died. One day she found her tiny little sandals and was playing with them, remembering Candy with great love and sadness. Just then her mom walked into the room and roughly took the sandals away from her, scolding her severely for playing with them. Jeanne felt as if she had done something terribly wrong, something that had to do with Candy's death and her own sorrow. Although she consciously forgot the event, it left a deep wound inside her that still affected her years later.

Through the word of knowledge, Lorraine was able to zero in on the key to unlock that pain. She and Jeanne prayed about the situation and gave it to the Lord. That day Jeanne was able to forgive her mother, and a healing over a long-standing situation occurred.

Connie

Another young woman, Connie, who was suffering from low self-image and rejection came for counseling. Recognizing the problem through the gift of knowledge, Lorraine tried to tell Connie that God really loved her, but Connie was unable to believe it. As Lorraine prayed, God gave her a picture of Jesus knocking at Connie's front door. She shared the picture with Connie and told her, "Jesus wants to come in and have breakfast with you."

"Oh, I can't let Him in," Connie insisted. "I'm in my bathrobe and curlers and I'm wearing a big sign on my back that says, 'Alcoholic.'"

Lorraine repeated, "He's knocking at your door, Connie. It's up to you to let Him in or He'll just wait or go away."

Finally Connie could picture herself letting Jesus into her house. In the Spirit, she heard Jesus tell her He loved her just the way she was. He took the sign with the word "alcoholic" written on it off her back and gave her a new name, "My little princess." He gave her a new robe to wear and told her He was healing her.

This was a turning point in Connie's life. She received faith and began to allow God to heal her.

The word of knowledge, revealing Connie's feelings about herself—alcoholic, unworthy, unacceptable of God's love—was the key used to set her free.

Dorothy

Dorothy's ex-husband was remarrying and their six-year-old daughter, Dottie, was going to be the flower girl at the wedding. Dorothy couldn't stand the thought of Dottie's being in the wedding and the fact that the child loved the new bride. Lorraine and Dorothy prayed and God showed Lorraine a diamond. The diamond had several facets to it that had not yet been cut. She told Dorothy that God wanted this diamond to be complete with every facet cut and reflecting the beauty that was potentially there. As they prayed, Dorothy saw this diamond as herself. Lorraine told Connie that she could cut the diamond by forgiving her husband and the new bride and by blessing them. It would be painful but there would be a new beauty reflecting from Dorothy's life. This picture gave Dorothy the key to setting herself free from the pain. It gave her faith to allow God to do the cutting. She wanted God's way, so in prayer she forgave and blessed her ex-husband and the new bride. Connie walked out of the counseling session a happy free woman.

Again, the gifts of the Holy Spirit in operation to do a quick work. In counseling the key may come as a word of knowledge; God may just drop a phrase into the counselor's heart, and by faith the counselor speaks it to the counselee. The key fits. Life and faith gush forth. God wants His children free.

Janet

God's specific word to another hurting daughter brought comfort and healing in a way that no other kind of counseling could .

The phone rang. It was my friend, Janet. She was sobbing so hard I could hardly understand her. Finally she got the words out. Jack, her childhood sweetheart and husband of 22 years, the father of her three children had announced that he was leaving her to live with a younger woman he had met at the office and fallen in love with. I knew that Janet had counseled many women who had faced this same trauma, but now it was happening to her. She didn't need a pat answer. She needed a fresh word from God.

In the natural I felt like saying, "Janet, all things work together for good," or "Now, Honey, have faith." But I knew she already knew the truth of these words. Janet's heart was broken. She needed to be comforted by the Holy Spirit. I said, "Janet, let me pray for you and I'll ask the Holy Spirit for a word of comfort. As I began to pray, her sobbing subsided and I could tell that God's peace was falling upon her. Yielding myself to the Holy Spirit and listening for the specific word from heaven for Janet, I heard these words in my spirit, "Janet, you are an Esther and I have already prepared you for this day and this trial. Lean not to your own understanding but take my hand and I will walk with you, guiding you each step of the way. You are no longer a Tamar, a victim, but I call you an Esther, one who was born for this time. As Esther was to her people, you are to your family. Trust Me. I have a good plan for your life."

Then the Lord had me quote Jeremiah 29:11: " 'For I know the plans I have for you,' declares the Lord, 'plans to prosper you and not to harm you, plans to give you hope and a future.' "

Those words from the Holy Spirit comforted Janet. The Lord had already spoken Jeremiah 29:11 to her during the previous week in her prayer time. She had always loved the story of Esther in the Bible. She admired Esther's courage and when the Lord called her an Esther, supernatural strength welled up inside her.

When she hung up the phone, Janet was different. She had heard from God; she had received His comfort and His strength.

Unique in God's eyes

God sees each one of us as unique individuals. He doesn't look at us and label us as Type A or Type B personalities. He doesn't have a list of problems we might face and then two or three scripture verses that will solve the problem. I'm afraid many Christian counselors limit God because they are ignorant of spiritual gifts. They have pat answers, even scriptures they recite to counselees. But God has supernatural gifts He wants His counselors to use. Only God knows the wounds, the strongholds of sin in a person's life. Very often the person being counseled doesn't have a clue as to why she's in pain or bondage. The Holy Spirit also has the key to set the counselee free. He will give that key to the one who asks.

Terri's healing

God often gives the key to the counselee. Two of us were praying and counseling with my friend, Terri, who was experiencing uncontrollable fear. As we waited on the Holy Spirit, Terri prayed, "Lord, show us the root, the circumstance that caused this fear in my life." Quickly, the Lord showed her a picture of a beating she endured from her abusive alcoholic dad when she was about four. Terri began to sob, releasing her pain to the Lord.

Then the Holy Spirit gave me a picture of several matadors who were wounding a bull with their swords. At first I didn't see any connection between the picture I was getting and what had happened so far. However, I have learned not to dismiss anything that comes when I pray, even though it may not seem relevant. I shared what I was seeing. Then I realized that the bull represented Terri's tenacity to stay alive and fight against those who would hurt her. The Lord showed me that the matadors who were trying to sneak up behind Terri and catch her off guard represented people in Terri's life that the enemy had used to try to destroy—even kill—her. The Lord showed Terri that two of the matadors were her mom and dad. Alcoholic and abusive, they had afflicted much pain and fear in her.

Much of Terri's life had been filled with abusive people. She had been married three times and her first two husbands were also alcoholic and abusive. Then a miracle happened. Terri heard about Jesus and became a strong Christian. In time she married a Christian man, Sam, a detective. They united their families and provided a Christian home for their six boys.

Tragedy struck again. One day Terri received the news, "Sam was shot to death today while he was arresting a suspected murderer." Terri was crushed, but as that bull with great tenacity she kept fighting. The death of her husband was another sword thrown at her, weakening but not destroying her.

As she raised her six boys by herself, the enemy had many more swords to attack her with, but Terri's bull-like tenacity carried her through.

As we counseled Terri that day and shared the supernatural pictures and word God was giving us, Terri was set free from the fear that had overwhelmed her. Now when she feels weak, the Lord flashes the picture of her as that great bull that will not be destroyed. She says, "Yes," in her heart, "that's who I am with Jesus and I will not give up."

Requirements of a counselor

If Christian counseling has made a significant change in your life, perhaps you feel you would like to "pass it on," and be a prayer counselor too. If you feel God is calling you to be a Christian counselor, seriously consider the following questions.

1. Are you in right relationship with the Lord, one who is able to hear His voice? A Christian counselor should be a mature Christian who trusts in the blood of Christ for cleansing from sin for herself and for her counselee. She should be one who knows God as a loving Father and who walks in grace.

2. Is your Christian life bathed in prayer? Prayer is the most important part of the counseling session, not something tacked on to the beginning or end of the sessions.

3. Are you dependent upon the Lord for guidance? Are you willing for the Holy Spirit to direct the sessions? A counselor must lay down her own agenda and her own understandings. One counselor told me that before she prays for someone the Lord has her read Psalm 1:1: *"How blessed is the man who does not walk in the counsel of the wicked."* She is very dependent on the Holy Spirit to guide her. She said He often gives her a word of knowledge by way of a picture, thoughts, or words. She has learned not to dismiss anything the Lord gives as it all has purpose and will come together as they continue to trust the Holy Spirit and pray.

4. Do you move in the gifts of the Spirit? As the counselor prays in the Spirit (in tongues) the gifts of the Spirit begin to flow. If the counselee objects to praying in tongues, the counselor can still pray silently. This stirs up the gifts. Faith and love are the two ingredients that allow the gifts to operate. Love for this counselee and love for God. Human love is not enough. A counselor must move in God's love. Ask God for His love. Faith will begin to flow to release the gifts.

As you counsel, expect the Holy Spirit to give you gifts. One counselor told me, "The Holy Spirit takes the weight of the burden off my shoulders as I trust in Him and His gifts in counseling.

Counseling by depending on the Holy Spirit and His gifts may be a new idea to you. Don't be afraid. You have the Holy Spirit in you to help you discern what is of God and what might not be.

My friend, Donna, a Spirit-filled lay counselor who counsels four days a week and has a long waiting list, says that she recently counseled a professional counselor. By the power of the Holy Spirit and His gifts, Donna was able to quickly uncover the root problems suffered by this counselor, and by prayer and deliverance Jesus set her free. She was overjoyed and *impressed.* She asked Donna if she could sit in on some of Donna's counseling sessions so that she could learn how the spiritual gifts work. From that time on, her counseling has changed to more dependence on the Holy Spirit and His gifts.

We live in a sinful world under the rule of Satan and none of us goes through life without being wounded in some way, some more than others. Although complete healing is available at our salvation, not everyone avails himself of it. Some need that extra touch from the Lord provided by Christian counseling before they can be whole.

Chapter Fourteen

The Spiritual Gifts in Deliverance

"He has sent me... to proclaim freedom for the captives and release from darkness for the prisoners" (Isa. 61: 1).

"And these signs will accompany those who believe: In my name they will drive out demons" (Mark 16:17).

"When Jesus had called the Twelve together, he gave them power and authority to drive out all demons" (Luke 9:1).

The line between releasing a person from the power of Satan through prayer and counseling and driving out an evil spirit is a very fine one. Most people who come for help are released very simply during prayer with others or while in a counseling session with no fanfare or manifestations. They become aware of their trauma and/or sin, ask forgiveness, extend forgiveness to the others involved, and are set free.

Abuses

During the early days of the Charismatic Renewal, we saw many abuses in the area of deliverance. Many people became convinced they had a demon. Deliverance ministries rose up in every city, and prayer and Bible study groups became "deliverance" groups. However, I thank God for those ministries. The church as a whole was ignorant of deliverance and spiritual warfare. However, it seems that when God brings a revelation to the surface, we as humans carry it to the extreme. That's what happened in the Charismatic Renewal. Today, I see much more balance in the area.

One of my close friends in ministry had what was known as a "deliverance ministry." Within a few years she was burned out and had to change her way of ministering. She explained that even though demons are behind the works of evil, our evil thoughts, actions, attitudes, etc., sometimes resisting the enemy by using our spiritual weapons — the blood of Jesus, the Name of Jesus, the Word of God, agreement in prayer, binding and loosing, fasting, praise and worship — is more effective than casting out the enemy. Using spiritual weapons also requires the one being prayed for to take more action and responsibility.

There are occasions, however, when the counselor or one praying must take authority over the spirits involved and, as Scripture says, "drive out the demons." (In my years of ministering in the gifts of the Spirit, I would say that this was true in only about 5% of the cases I ministered in.)

Release from a spirit of fear

Let me share a personal experience of being delivered from a spirit of fear. Many years ago several times a week, I had to turn off the lights in the gym at the school where my husband was basketball coach. Now, I wasn't a coward; in fact, very much the opposite, but I usually did this while people were leaving so I wouldn't be alone in the dark. One night, however, everyone left early and I was alone. Coming back down the dark hall to our apartment, I was terrorized.

My roommates in college had tried to get me over my fear. One night they told me they would walk around the block in one direction, and I was to walk the other way and meet them half way. We started out but as soon as they turned the corner, fear engulfed me. I ran back to the dorm the way I had come as fast as I could. My heart was beating so fast that I was short of breath, but not from running. My roommates didn't understand the cause of this extreme fear. They laughed and I joined in, but inside I was crying and wondering why I had overreacted.

Years later at a prayer meeting, I shared my fear of the dark. My friends began to pray. One said, "God shows me you have a *spirit* of fear." The rest of the group agreed and they prayed for me to be delivered. They took authority over the evil spirit and demanded it to release me. After they prayed I felt such joy. A warmth of God's love surrounded me, and I felt as light as a feather. I hadn't foamed at the mouth, gotten thrown to the floor, or screamed out, but I knew something had left. I was free. To this day 25 years later, I am still free of that paralyzing fear. If I am in a dark place and fear starts to grip me, I quote the promises of God in His Word, *"Fear not. I will never leave you nor forsake you"* (Heb. 13:5 KJV). Or I call out for warrior angels to protect me. *"Are not all angels ministering spirits sent to serve those who will inherit salvation?"* (Heb. 1:14).

You may ask how this evil spirit got an inroad in my life. Perhaps it was during a traumatic time when I was a child living in the slums. My alcoholic parents fought a lot and my abusive dad also beat my mother. I was especially afraid of men. One day I saw a drunk man walking toward our apartment. I didn't have time to do anything but hide behind the front door, hoping he would come in and go upstairs. But he sat down on the step right in front of me. He couldn't see me, but my little heart beat wildly as I crouched behind that door. This type of trauma allows a spirit of fear to come in. When my prayer group prayed, the spirit left and the Holy Spirit filled the area where the demon spirit had been.

A few years ago while I was driving in a rather secluded area, my car suddenly lost all power on a bridge that had no shoulder. Not only did the motor stop running, but the lights went out. It was late at night, very dark and raining. Fear started to rise up in me.

"No one will be able to see my car without lights – they'll crash right into me," I thought. I decided to try to find help. The first two cars that stopped reeked with alcohol. One man offered to take me to a gas station. I refused, but fear began to really manifest itself. I got back into my car and prayed, "Lord, you said I wasn't supposed to be afraid, but this is terrible. I'm afraid. Help, Lord."

Within seconds a patrol car pulled up to help. Fear in this instance was a warning to ask God for help and He sent it by way of the patrolman. Had I not been delivered of the spirit of fear this experience might have had a different ending. Praise God for deliverance.

Reluctance to driving out demons

In those cases where people are demonized, we find many Christians very reluctant to cast out the demons. I believe this is mainly for four reasons:

1. They are ignorant about demons and what the Word of God says about their work.

2. They attribute much more power to demons than Scripture gives them, and they are afraid the demons will retaliate and harm the one who is praying.

3. They lack the assurance of the authority Jesus gave us when He instructed us to cast out demons. (They may not have seen other Christians demonstrate this power and authority.)

4. They are afraid of the manifestations: foaming at the mouth, writhing on the floor, or ungodly screaming. Yes, sometimes, (and I emphasize the *sometimes*) these manifestations do occur, but again, very infrequently.

Ministering in Russia

Recently while ministering with my friend, Paula Shields, in Moscow and other cities in Russia, I noticed a sadness in the eyes of many believers. Since Paula had ministered in Russia on several occasions, I asked her about it. She said, "Fran, many of these church leaders need deliverance." For 80 years under communist rule, most Russian people did not hear the gospel. Whenever there is a void, the enemy eagerly fills it with his devices, mainly the practice of witchcraft and psychic phenomena. When we offered to pray for these leaders, they eagerly signed up because they knew they were being harassed by demons. They had also seen what deliverance prayers had accomplished in other leaders and heard their testimonies. I didn't hear anyone discussing, "Can a believer have a demon?" I heard, "Will you set me free? Will you cast out any demon you discern?"

When we prayed, I did sometimes see foaming at the mouth, writhing on the floor, and loud screaming as the demons left. At first I was a little shaken by the display of the enemy. I often quoted the scripture, *"He that is in me is greater than he that is in the world"* (1 John 4:4 KJV). I needed to believe and strengthen myself with those words and the authority Jesus has given us.

Scripture teaches much about deliverance but until we are in a situation where we are challenged, it may be only head knowledge.

My Lutheran friends, the Torvics, missionaries to Madagascar, said they were never taught how to cast out demons in Bible school, but before they ate one meal on the mission field, they were challenged by a demon-possessed native. They soon learned that God had anointed them not only to preach but to cast out demons and heal the sick. They told me, "We didn't really believe in demons when we went out, but we sure do now."

How the gifts are used in deliverance

The gift of discerning of spirits is probably the spiritual gift most often given by the Holy Spirit to detect the kind of spirit that is harassing, oppressing, or possessing a person. A second gift, the word of knowledge, is another key gift. Often the word of knowledge will come by way of a picture, an impression, or a supernatural knowing within the person praying. Knowing how to pray and knowing which weapon will work most effectively is given through a word of wisdom by the Holy Spirit. When God gives a gift of this kind, it is like a sharp-shooter hitting the target, instead of a shot gun blast that comes close to the target but doesn't hit the bull's eye.

Along with the spiritual gifts, we have the whole arsenal of spiritual weapons, mentioned earlier, for our use. These are mighty weapons with which we can destroy the works of the devil. As in all ministry, learning to recognize the voice of the Lord is crucial. Many mistakes have been made because of the lack of hearing God's voice correctly.

My first experience

The first time I was involved with deliverance was in a church where I was teaching. The group was singing spiritual choruses when a woman began to cough loudly. The veins on her neck bulged and her tongue hung out. At first I thought she was choking on something, but the Lord told me it was demon activity. With very little faith, I took authority over the demon. At first, nothing happened, so I told the group to sing, "Oh, the blood of Jesus." As they sang, the woman recovered. After the meeting I spoke with her, and she told me she had known she needed deliverance. That was why she had come to the meeting.

Some more experiences

My friend, Linda, a counselor, shared several abbreviated accounts of some of her experiences (with the permission of the people involved).

While counseling with a woman, Linda saw a pressure, like hands pressing in, around the woman's head. She asked the woman if she had a headache. The woman said she'd had one for the better part of 12 years, ever since she'd had an abortion. Linda discerned a strong spirit of murder in the woman. After some counseling, the woman confessed her sin and asked forgiveness, Linda took authority over the spirit of murder and the woman was freed.

While working with another counselee, Linda saw a picture of a mummy in the back seat of a car. When she asked the woman about it, the woman said, "That's my husband. The car is where we have our worst arguments. I've often wished him dead." Linda discerned a spirit of death. After the woman confessed her sin, asked God for forgiveness, and in turn forgave her husband, Linda cast out the spirit of death and the woman went home a free woman.

Another woman came to Linda because she wanted to ask her mother who was living with her to find a place of her own, but she was terrorized of her. While they prayed, the woman remembered that when she was a child her mother had frequently controlled her with the threat, "If you don't behave yourself, I'll kill myself." Although she wasn't conscious of it, she held much rage and anger against her mother. After she confessed her sin and forgave her mother, Linda took authority over this spirit of terror. The woman was set free and has never been afraid of her mother since.

Soul ties

Many people are bound to someone by soul ties, especially when there has been sexual activity or perversion involved. These soul ties must be broken before the person is truly free to love another.

A husband and wife came to Linda. Although the couple loved one another, the wife felt she had never really been in her husband's heart. As they counseled, the husband revealed that in high school, he had been in love with a girl, although they hadn't been sexually intimate. When she went off as a volunteer missionary, he vowed he would wait for her. However, when she returned home, she didn't contact him and married someone else. Deeply hurt, he never dealt with his pain. In the counseling session, the power of the vow was broken and the soul tie to the young woman severed. Now the man was free to truly love his wife.

An empty house

It is dangerous to pray deliverance for someone who is not ready to be delivered. Many people who come for deliverance only want temporary relief; they aren't ready to change their life styles. Remember Jesus' words: "*When an evil spirit comes out of a man, it goes through arid places seeking rest and does not find it. Then it says, 'I will return to the house I left.' When it arrives, it finds the house unoccupied, swept clean, and put in order. Then it goes and takes with it seven other spirits more wicked than itself and they go in and live there. And the final condition of that man is worse than the first*" (Matt. 12: 43-45).

Whenever I speak on abuse, there are usually demonic manifestations. One time when I was speaking in Poulsbo, Washington, a woman brought an unwilling friend to the meeting. Suddenly, in the middle of the meeting, she fell to the floor, writhing, arching her back, and stiffening her neck. I silenced the demon, but when I asked the woman if she wanted deliverance, she said she wasn't ready yet, so I didn't try to deliver her. This story has a happy ending, however. Several months later I saw her, and she was completely delivered. When she was ready for help, she received it.

We do not need to be afraid of demons. Jesus has given us the power to take authority over them: "Greater *is he that is in you than he that is in the world.*" While we shouldn't go around looking for demons to drive out, remember that when the occasion calls for it, we have been commissioned to take the authority given us in the Name of Jesus and set the captives free.

Epilogue

My hope is that this book has challenged you into action, not merely given you head knowledge. The nine gifts of the Spirit: tongues, interpretation, prophecy, word of knowledge, word of wisdom, discerning of spirits, healing, miracles and faith (1 Cor. 12: 7-11) are God's tools given to us to co-labor with Him. First Corinthians 12:7 says, *"the manifestation of the Spirit is given to every man (men, women, children) to profit withal"* (KJV).

God desires to manifest His love, His power, His glory, His wisdom through you and me. How does this happen?

1. By knowing Him. By recognizing His voice and obeying it. This is an ongoing process.

2. By knowing His Word, the Bible.

3. By loving Him and allowing Him to love you back.

4. By living in grace and mercy, not legalism.

5. By being baptized in the Holy Spirit and using your spiritual language (tongues) to build yourself up so you can build others up.

In his book **Bold Love** Dr. Dan B. Allender says, "Whatever has the potential to do good has an equal, if not greater, possibility of doing damage. If that is true with the Word of God, which has been used to justify war, persecution, inquisitions, torture, and strife, then how much more of a possibility with mere human words."[1]

I realize the potential for harm as I encourage all God's people to "desire spiritual gifts." There will always be some who will operate in the human spirit or a hellish spirit but most will minister in the Holy Spirit. Let us not be afraid of Satan and his tactics but let us press on to maturity. You can be a vessel co-laboring with God to bring about His manifest presence — His glory filling the earth.

Notes

[1]Dan B. Allender and Dr. Tremper Longman III, *Bold Love*, *(Colorado Springs: NavPress, 1992), p. 311.*